TARUN TAKSHAY

Scale 10X Google Ads Secrets

TAKSHAY
DIGITAL ACADEMY

First edition

ISBN: 978-93-344-1500-1

This book was professionally typeset on Reedsy.
Find out more at reedsy.com

To Lord Krishna —

the divine strategist, the eternal mentor, and the voice of the Gita.

May this work be an offering of gratitude for the clarity and courage You inspire in me.

And to my beloved parents —

whose love, sacrifices, and prayers built the foundation upon which I stand today.

Finally, to my readers —

May this book serve as both a guide and a reminder that your knowledge, when combined with systems and faith, has the power to create freedom, impact, and legacy.

"Success in digital marketing isn't about spending more, it's about thinking smarter. Every ad is a seed — plant it right, and it can grow into a forest of opportunities."

Contents

Foreword

The world of entrepreneurship has changed forever. Today, the businesses that thrive are not always the ones with the biggest offices, largest teams, or deepest pockets — they are the ones that know how to capture attention and turn it into trust.

Google Ads is one of the most powerful tools of our time. It gives every entrepreneur, no matter how big or small, the ability to place their idea directly in front of someone who is already searching for it. That's not just marketing — that's opportunity.

But let's be honest: for many, Google Ads feels overwhelming. Complicated dashboards, confusing metrics, wasted budgets — it's no wonder so many give up before they ever see results. And yet, those who stick with it and master the system often transform their businesses entirely.

That is why this book was written. *Google Ads Secrets* is not just a manual on ads; it is a roadmap for entrepreneurs who want clarity in a world of noise. It's designed to take you from feeling uncertain about where your money goes, to confidently investing in campaigns that bring measurable results.

More than strategies and tools, this book is about a mindset: test, learn, refine, and scale. It's about seeing ads not as expenses, but as investments — investments into your growth, your visibility, and your mission.

As you begin this journey, remember this: every click has the potential to change your business, and every ad you run is a seed planted for your future.

Nurture it with wisdom, and the rewards will multiply.

This is your opportunity to stop guessing, stop struggling, and start mastering. Welcome to *Google Ads Secrets*. Your next level as an entrepreneur starts here.

Tarun Takshay

Founder, *Takshay Digital Academy*

Preface

When I first started running Google Ads, I wasted money. A lot of it. I remember staring at the dashboard, confused by all the numbers, trying to figure out why nothing was working. Maybe you've been there too.

The truth is, Google Ads can feel overwhelming at first. But once I cracked the code — understanding how to structure campaigns, choose the right keywords, write compelling ads, and track results — everything changed. My campaigns became predictable, profitable, and scalable.

This book isn't just about theory. It's about real-world lessons, strategies, and insights I've gathered from years of trial and error, testing, and eventually mastering this powerful platform. I've written it in a way that feels like we're having a conversation — because I want you to feel supported on this journey.

By the time you finish this book, you'll not only understand Google Ads — you'll be able to launch campaigns that actually make money. And if you want to go deeper, I've paired this book with a special combo course that gives you behind-the-scenes training, templates, and step-by-step walk through.

Acknowledgments

No book is ever created in isolation, and *Google Ads Secrets* is no exception. This journey has been shaped by the love, support, and inspiration of so many people who stood beside me.

First and foremost, I bow in gratitude to my Lord Krishna. Your guidance, strength, and blessings have carried me through every challenge and every victory. Without your presence in my heart, none of this would have been possible.

To my family — thank you for your patience, understanding, and unwavering belief in me. Your love has been my anchor during long nights, endless writing, and the countless trials of entrepreneurship.

To my mentors, who showed me the power of systems and mindset — your wisdom gave me the courage to step forward and share my own path with others.

To my students at **Takshay Digital Academy** — you are my daily inspiration. Watching you take action, grow, and transform your businesses gave me the drive to create this book. Every page carries lessons born from our shared journey.

And finally, to every entrepreneur who has dared to dream bigger — this book is for you. May it give you clarity where there is confusion, hope where there is doubt, and results where there have only been struggles.

With deepest gratitude,

Tarun Takshay

Prologue

When I first stepped into the world of digital marketing, I felt exactly what many of you may be feeling right now — excitement mixed with confusion. The promise of reaching thousands of people through a single campaign was thrilling. But the reality of navigating dashboards, settings, and endless options was overwhelming.

Like many entrepreneurs, I made mistakes. I spent money without clear strategies, ran ads that brought traffic but no sales, and sometimes wondered if Google Ads really worked at all. Those moments were frustrating, even discouraging. But looking back, they were also the turning points. Because every mistake became a lesson, and every failure forced me to dig deeper, learn smarter, and refine my approach.

Over time, I discovered that Google Ads is not just about keywords and budgets. It's about understanding human behavior, aligning with intent, and building systems that work even while you sleep. Once I cracked that code, everything changed — not only for my own business, but for my students at **Takshay Digital Academy**, who began applying these secrets to achieve results of their own.

This book, *Google Ads Secrets,* is born from that journey. It carries the lessons I learned the hard way so you don't have to. It is both a guide and a companion — something to help you navigate the complexity with confidence and clarity.

As you begin this book, I invite you to approach it not just as a marketer, but as an entrepreneur. Because at the end of the day, ads are not about clicks;

they are about connections. And every connection you make has the power to change your business — and maybe even your life.

So let's begin this journey together. By the time you reach the final page, I hope you not only understand how to run Google Ads, but also feel empowered to use them as a tool to grow your vision, your impact, and your legacy.

Tarun Takshay

Founder, *Takshay Digital Academy*

Introduction

In today's digital world, visibility is no longer optional — it is survival. Whether you are a coach, entrepreneur, or small business owner, your success depends on one simple truth: if people can't find you, they can't buy from you.

That is where **Google Ads** comes in.

Think about it: every single day, billions of people type their thoughts, problems, and needs directly into Google. Unlike traditional advertising, where you interrupt people with your message, Google Ads allows you to appear exactly when someone is already looking for what you offer. It is not just advertising — it is *intent-driven marketing*.

And yet, despite its power, many entrepreneurs struggle with Google Ads. They see it as complicated, risky, or too expensive. Some try it once, waste money, and walk away convinced that "ads don't work." The truth is not that Google Ads don't work — it's that most people never learned how to use them the right way.

This book was created to change that.

In *Google Ads Secrets*, you will discover the proven strategies, frameworks, and insider techniques that transform Google Ads from a confusing platform into a predictable system for growth. You'll learn how to:

- Choose the right campaigns and targeting without wasting money

- Craft ad copy that captures attention and drives action
- Optimize budgets so you pay less and earn more
- Track, measure, and scale results with confidence

But more than tools and tactics, this book will also help you develop the right mindset — to treat ads not as expenses, but as investments into your business and future.

As you move through these chapters, remember: success with Google Ads does not come from chasing hacks or shortcuts. It comes from clarity, strategy, and consistent execution.

So take a deep breath, let go of the overwhelm, and get ready to master one of the most powerful opportunities of our time. By the end of this book, you won't just "run ads" — you'll know how to build a system that brings leads, sales, and growth on demand.

Welcome to *Google Ads Secrets*. Let's begin.

Tarun Takshay
Founder, *Takshay Digital Academy*

1

Book Summary: Google Ads Mastery

From Clicks to Clients

Most businesses don't fail because they lack a great product or service. They fail because they can't consistently bring in the right customers.

That's where **Google Ads** comes in. Done right, it's the most powerful, intent-driven traffic source on the planet. Done wrong, it's a money pit.

In *Google Ads Mastery,* Tarun pulls back the curtain on the exact frameworks, strategies, and systems he's used to turn ads into predictable profit machines for himself and his clients. Written with a mix of professional insight and personal experience, this book is both a step-by-step guide and a mentor-in-your-pocket.

What You'll Discover Inside:

- **Foundations** — Why Google Ads is different, the psychology of search intent, and how to identify your premium client avatar.
- **Crafting High-Performance Ads** — The anatomy of a high-converting ad, storytelling with headlines and extensions, and the visual power of YouTube and Display.
- **Targeting & Strategy** — Keyword research, retargeting, funnel mapping, and smart budgeting that stops wasted spend.
- **Optimization & Scaling** — How to read data, run simple A/B tests, and scale campaigns without burning cash.
- **Advanced Playbook** — Evergreen campaign structures, cross-channel integrations with Meta and email, and the rise of AI & automation.
- **Beyond Ads** — Building a team, staying compliant, and transforming ads into long-term acquisition systems.

What Makes This Book Different?

Unlike generic guides, this book includes:

- **Personal stories** from real campaigns (wins and mistakes).
- **Case studies** across eCommerce, local business, coaching, and SaaS.
- **Action steps and worksheets** at the end of each chapter so you make progress as you read.
- **Swipe files, checklists, and templates** you can apply immediately.

Who This Book Is For:

- Entrepreneurs tired of "guessing" with ads.
- Marketers who want a proven system to scale.
- Coaches, consultants, eCom owners, or local business operators ready to attract premium clients.
- Anyone who wants to stop wasting money on traffic and start turning

ads into clients.

2

Why Google Ads Are the Most Intent-Driven Traffic Source

When I first discovered Google Ads, I thought it was just another advertising platform. I had already tried running social media ads, boosting posts, and experimenting with different channels. Sometimes I got clicks, sometimes likes, but what I didn't get consistently were paying customers.

The problem? Most platforms focus on *interruption*. You're putting ads in front of people while they're scrolling through memes, videos, or their cousin's vacation photos. They didn't wake up wanting to buy what you're offering. They were there to be entertained — and you're just hoping to catch their attention.

Google Ads is different.

And that difference completely changed the way I saw online marketing.

The Power of Intent

Think about it: when someone types into Google, they're not there by accident. They're actively *looking* for something. A problem. A solution. A product. A service.

- When someone types *"best chiropractor near me,"* they're not looking for funny TikToks. They're in pain, and they want help now.
- When someone searches *"top project management software,"* they're not browsing for fun. They're ready to compare, evaluate, and potentially buy.
- When someone types *"emergency plumber open 24/7,"* that's not curiosity — that's urgency.

This is what I call **the intent factor** — and no other platform gives you access to it at the same scale as Google.

My Turning Point with Intent Marketing

I'll be honest: in the beginning, I wasted money. My first campaigns were disasters — broad keywords, random ad copy, no tracking. I thought throwing money at Google would magically bring clients.

Instead, I burned through hundreds of dollars with nothing to show for it.

But the moment I shifted my mindset to **understanding search intent**, everything changed.
I stopped targeting everyone.
I stopped chasing vanity metrics.
I started asking: *What is this person actually looking for at the exact moment they type this into Google?*

That simple shift — from chasing traffic to aligning with intent — turned my campaigns from a gamble into a predictable system. Suddenly, I wasn't just getting clicks. I was getting **qualified leads and real paying customers.**

Why This Matters for You

If you're reading this, chances are you've tried other forms of marketing. Maybe you've posted content that nobody saw. Maybe you've run social ads that got likes but no sales. Or maybe you've been skeptical about ads altogether.

Here's the truth: once you understand intent-driven marketing, you'll never look at advertising the same way again.

Google Ads gives you the ability to:

- **Show up at the exact moment** your customer is searching.
- **Filter out the noise** of people who aren't ready to buy.
- **Turn ad spend into investment**, because every dollar is targeting people with intent.

That's why I call Google Ads the **most predictable and scalable traffic source** for businesses — from solopreneurs to global brands.

A Preview of What's Ahead

In this book, I'm going to share the exact frameworks I've developed over years of running campaigns — the same ones I use in my consulting and inside my premium course. You'll learn how to:

- Identify high-intent keywords that bring in the right clients.
- Craft ads that speak directly to what your prospects are searching for.
- Build campaigns that don't just get clicks, but generate measurable ROI.

By the end, you won't just know *why* Google Ads works. You'll know exactly *how* to use it to grow your business predictably.

And here's my promise: I'll teach you in a way that's clear, actionable, and free of jargon — because I remember what it was like being lost in dashboards and acronyms.

This first chapter is your mindset shift. From here on, we're not chasing attention anymore. We're aligning with intent — and that's the foundation of everything you'll learn in the chapters ahead.

Action Steps: Your First Intent Shift

1 Reflect on Your Audience's Intent

- Write down 3 search phrases your ideal client might type into Google *right before* they buy your product or service.
- Example: instead of "marketing tips," think "best digital marketing agency near me."

2 Identify Your Current Traffic Sources

- Ask yourself: are you currently relying on interruption-based platforms (like social media), or intent-driven platforms (like Google)?
- Note where most of your best leads have come from so far.

3 Mindset Shift Exercise

- Complete this sentence in your notebook:
- *"When someone searches for [keyword/phrase], what they really want is ___________."*
- This will help you start thinking like your customer, not just an advertiser.

4 Quick Win

- Go to Google right now and type in a keyword your potential customer might search.
- Look at the ads that appear.
- Ask: *Do these ads speak to my intent? If not, how could I write one better?*

3

Understanding the Google Ads Ecosystem

When I first opened the Google Ads dashboard, I remember feeling like I had walked into the cockpit of an airplane. Buttons everywhere. Tabs, charts, and metrics I didn't understand.

I thought to myself: *"Do I really need to master all of this just to run one ad?"*

The truth? No.

You don't need to master *everything* — you just need to understand the **Google Ads ecosystem** and how the pieces fit together. Once I figured out what each campaign type was designed for, I stopped wasting money on the wrong ads and started choosing the right tools for the job.

Think of it like this: if Google Ads is a toolbox, then Search, Display, YouTube, and Shopping are the tools. Each one has a purpose. Use the wrong tool, and you'll struggle. Use the right one, and things just click.

The Four Core Campaign Types You Need to Know

1. Search Ads (The Workhorse)

These are the ads that show up when someone types a query into Google. They're text-based and intent-driven.

- Example: "best divorce lawyer near me."
- Why it matters: You're catching people at the exact moment they're searching.
- My story: Once I shifted my budget from display (which was too broad for my service business at the time) to search ads, I immediately started seeing leads roll in. It was like flipping a switch from *hope marketing* to *predictable lead flow*.

2. Display Ads (The Billboard)

These are visual banner ads that appear across Google's partner sites. They're great for building awareness or retargeting, but not always for direct conversions.

- Example: You look at a pair of shoes online, then later see them advertised while reading the news.
- Why it matters: Display is more about visibility and brand recall. I use it heavily for remarketing because it's like a gentle nudge to people who already know me.

3. YouTube Ads (The Storyteller)

Owned by Google, YouTube lets you run video ads before, during, or after videos.

- Example: A 30-second video ad before a tutorial someone searched for.
- Why it matters: It's a hybrid of intent (people searching for "how to fix

back pain") and interruption (ads showing up mid-video). Done right, YouTube lets you build trust faster because video creates connection.

- My experience: The first time I ran a YouTube ad, I thought nobody would watch it. But the engagement shocked me — it pulled in leads who later said, "I felt like I already knew you from your video."

4. Shopping Ads (The Storefront)

These are the product ads with images, prices, and links that appear when people search for physical products.

- Example: Searching for "Nike Air Max 2025" and seeing a grid of products with images and prices.
- Why it matters: Perfect for e-commerce businesses. If you sell products, Shopping Ads give you a front-row seat in Google's marketplace.
- Note: Even if you don't sell physical products, it's important to know these exist — because your competitors might.

How They Work Together

The real magic happens when you **combine campaigns strategically**.

- A prospect sees your **Search Ad** → clicks your site.
- They leave without buying → your **Display Ad** follows them around.
- They go on YouTube → your video ad reminds them of the value you offer.
- If you sell products → Shopping Ads show them exactly what they want to buy.

That's not "random advertising." That's a system. And once you see it as an ecosystem, you'll stop treating campaigns like isolated experiments and start using them as parts of a predictable machine.

My Big Lesson Here

The biggest mistake I made early on? Trying to do everything at once.

I spread my budget across Search, Display, and YouTube without a clear strategy. That meant a little money went everywhere, and nothing worked.

What I should have done — and what I recommend for you — is to **start with Search Ads** (because intent is highest there), then expand into Display and YouTube once you've got predictable results.

Master one channel first. Then add the others like gears in a machine.

Action Steps: Your Ecosystem Map

Identify Your Primary Campaign Type

- Ask: Which type of ad makes the most sense for my business right now?
- Services → Start with **Search Ads**.
- Products → Lean into **Shopping Ads**.
- Personal brand or content-driven → Add **YouTube Ads** later.

Draw Your Funnel Flow

- Sketch (on paper or digital):
- Where will you capture attention? (Search, YouTube, or Display)
- Where will you retarget? (Display, YouTube)
- How will you close the sale? (Landing page, Shopping Ad, etc.)

Choose ONE Campaign to Launch First

- Write down: *"My first campaign will be ________ because my customers are most likely searching/seeing me on ________."*

Quick Win

- Open Google and search for a keyword your customers might use.
- Look at which types of ads appear (Search, Shopping, maybe even YouTube suggestions).
- This exercise will show you where your competitors are already playing.

4

The Psychology of Search Intent

One of the most important lessons I learned with Google Ads didn't come from staring at dashboards. It came from sitting across the table from real customers.

I used to obsess over keywords, CPC bids, and ad formats — but I was missing the bigger picture: **what was going on in the customer's mind at the exact moment they typed their search into Google?**

That's when I realized:

Google Ads is not about chasing clicks. It's about understanding intent.

If you can step inside your customer's head and decode their intent, you'll never waste money on irrelevant clicks again.

What Is Search Intent?

Search intent is the "why" behind a search. It's the reason someone types a specific phrase into Google.

There are three main levels of intent you must master:

1. Informational Intent (The Researcher)
These users are curious but not ready to buy.

- Example: *"How to fix lower back pain"*
- They're seeking information, tutorials, or answers.
- As an advertiser, your role is to **educate and build trust**, not push the sale immediately.

2. Commercial/Comparative Intent (The Evaluator)
These users are considering their options.

- Example: *"Best chiropractor near me"* or *"Top project management software 2025"*
- They're not just researching; they're comparing providers or products.
- This is where your ad copy should highlight **differentiators, credibility, and trust signals**.

3. Transactional Intent (The Buyer)
These users are ready to take action.

- Example: *"Book emergency plumber near me"*
- They've already decided to buy — they just need the right solution at the right time.
- This is where **clear CTAs, urgency, and easy booking/purchase flows** win the sale.

My Big Mistake With Intent

Early in my journey, I lumped all keywords together.

I treated *"how to fix back pain"* the same way as *"book chiropractor near me."*

Result? I got clicks, but almost no conversions.

I was paying for people who wanted free information, not services.

When I started separating my campaigns by intent level, everything changed. I built funnels that *matched where the customer was mentally*, instead of pushing a one-size-fits-all ad.

- Informational = blog content + lead magnets.
- Comparative = testimonial ads + differentiators.
- Transactional = strong offers + booking page.

That's when my campaigns stopped feeling like "throwing spaghetti at the wall" and started producing predictable results.

The Intent Funnel Framework

Think of Google Ads as an **intent funnel**:

Top of Funnel (TOFU): Informational Intent

- Goal: Capture attention & build authority.
- Ad Strategy: Content promotion, YouTube how-to videos, Display ads for awareness.

Middle of Funnel (MOFU): Comparative Intent

- Goal: Nurture trust & stand out.
- Ad Strategy: Search campaigns for "best/top" keywords, case studies, strong ad extensions.

Bottom of Funnel (BOFU): Transactional Intent

- Goal: Convert leads into paying customers.
- Ad Strategy: High-intent keywords ("buy," "book," "near me"), Shopping ads, retargeting campaigns.

If you align your campaigns with these stages, you're not just running ads. You're building a system that meets customers exactly where they are.

The Emotional Layer of Intent

Intent isn't just logic — it's emotion. Behind every search is a feeling:

- Pain (back pain, plumbing emergencies, financial stress)
- Desire (new shoes, career growth, better body)
- Curiosity (learning a skill, exploring options)

The better you can connect your ad copy to that **emotional driver**, the higher your click-through rates and conversions will be.

When I stopped writing "features" and started writing to the *feeling behind the search*, my ads started winning.

- Instead of: *"Chiropractic sessions available"*
- I wrote: *"End Back Pain Fast — Book Your Same-Day Appointment."*

See the difference? One lists a service. The other speaks to the intent and emotion.

My Takeaway for You

Never look at keywords as just words. Look at them as **windows into your customer's mind**.

Every search tells a story. If you can decode it, you'll never struggle to find customers online again.

Action Steps: Decoding Your Customer's Intent

List 5 Keywords for Each Intent Stage

- Informational: What questions would they ask?
- Comparative: What "best/top/near me" searches would they make?
- Transactional: What urgent or purchase-ready terms would they use?

Map Your Funnel

- Draw a 3-stage funnel: TOFU, MOFU, BOFU.
- Place your keywords under the right stage.

Rewrite One Ad With Emotion

- Pick one transactional keyword.
- Rewrite an ad headline or description to focus on the *feeling* behind the search, not just the service.

Quick Win

- Search your own keywords on Google.
- Ask: Do the ads showing up actually match the intent? If not, that's your opportunity to stand out.

5

Crafting Your Premium Client Avatar for Paid Traffic

When I first started running ads, I thought more traffic meant more business. My logic was simple: if 1,000 people saw my ad, that had to be better than 100 people, right?

Wrong.

What I quickly discovered was that traffic is not the goal. **The right traffic is the goal.**

And that's where most advertisers get it wrong — they focus on getting in front of *everyone*, instead of focusing on the right *someone*.

The truth?

Google Ads will happily take your money and show your ads to thousands of people. But unless you know *exactly* who you want to attract, you'll burn through your budget fast.

That's why you need to create your **Premium Client Avatar** — a clear picture of your dream customer, the one who sees your ad and thinks: *"This is exactly what I've been looking for."*

Why "Premium" Clients Matter

Not all customers are equal.

- Some will haggle, drain your time, and never be satisfied.
- Others will happily pay premium prices, value your expertise, and refer you to their network.

When I stopped trying to target *everyone* and started focusing on *premium clients only*, everything changed:

- My ad spend dropped because I wasn't wasting clicks on unqualified leads.
- My close rates went up because my ads spoke directly to the right people.
- My business felt lighter because I was working with clients who valued my services.

This is the shift I want you to make: stop chasing "anyone" and start designing your campaigns for the **someone** you want most.

The Four Pillars of a Premium Client Avatar

To define your Premium Client Avatar, answer these four questions:

1. **Who Are They? (Demographics & Basics)**

- Age, gender, location
- Income level, education, job role
- Do they live in a city or suburb?

Example: *35-year-old marketing manager, mid-sized company, located in Austin,*

TX.

2. What Do They Want? (Goals & Desires)

- What outcome are they chasing?
- What would success look like for them?

Example: *They want to generate leads without wasting money on social ads.*

3. What Keeps Them Up at Night? (Pain Points & Fears)

- What problems frustrate them?
- What do they want to avoid at all costs?

Example: *They're tired of hiring agencies that overpromise and underdeliver. They fear wasting their limited budget.*

4. Where Do They Search? (Digital Behavior & Intent)

- What keywords would they use?
- Are they searching locally, nationally, or globally?
- Do they compare competitors before deciding?

Example: *Searches "Google Ads consultant near me" and "best PPC expert for small business."*

The Psychology of the Avatar

Your Premium Client Avatar isn't just about data — it's about *mindset*. You need to step into their shoes and ask:

- What triggers them to search?

- What emotional state are they in? (frustrated, hopeful, urgent?)
- What do they secretly wish someone would say to them?

When I started writing ads that sounded like I was reading my client's mind, my click-through rates doubled. People don't click because you listed features. They click because you showed them you **understand their problem better than anyone else.**

My Personal Shift

At one point, I was targeting "small business owners." That sounded smart — broad audience, more reach. But in reality, it was too vague. A yoga studio owner in Miami does not think or buy the same way as a B2B SaaS founder in New York.

When I narrowed my focus to "service-based businesses spending at least $1,000/month on marketing," suddenly my ads clicked. My messaging got sharper. My results got better.

That's the power of a Premium Client Avatar: **clarity creates conversions.**

Action Steps: Build Your Premium Client Avatar

Create a Profile

- Give your avatar a name (e.g., "Marketing Manager Mike" or "Busy Mom Sarah").
- Write a one-paragraph summary of who they are, what they want, and what they fear.

Define 3 Core Search Phrases

- What are three things they would type into Google when actively looking for your solution?

Pain & Desire List

- Write down 3 pains they want to escape and 3 desires they want to achieve.
- Example: *Pain = wasting money on bad ads. Desire = steady flow of quality leads.*

Quick Win

- Test your avatar: Go to Google and type in one of their search phrases. Look at the ads.
- Ask: *Would my avatar click these ads? If not, what would I write instead?*

6

The Anatomy of a High-Converting Search Ad

I'll never forget the first time one of my ads hit a **10/10 Quality Score**. I had been fumbling with average ads for months, paying higher CPCs than my competitors. Then one day, I wrote an ad so aligned with the keyword and the customer's intent that it just worked. Higher CTR, lower CPC, and actual conversions rolling in.

That's when I realized: writing Google Ads isn't about stuffing keywords. It's about **structuring every line with intent and psychology in mind.**

The Three Parts of a Search Ad

Every Google Search Ad has 3 core elements:

1. Headlines (The Hook)

- You get up to 3 headlines, each up to 30 characters.
- These are the first thing people see — the "scroll stopper" of Google Ads.
- Example of weak headline: *"Best Lawyer Services."*

- Example of strong headline: *"Win Your Case — Book a Free Consult."*
- Tip: Include the **keyword** in the headline + one **emotional trigger** (relief, speed, fear, desire).

2. Descriptions (The Persuasion)

- You get up to 2 descriptions, each up to 90 characters.
- This is where you move from grabbing attention to building trust.
- Example of weak description: *"We offer legal services in your area."*
- Example of strong description: *"Over 20 Years Experience. Same-Day Appointments Available. Call Now."*
- Tip: Use benefits, credibility markers (years in business, reviews, guarantees), and urgency.

3. Display Path (The Reassurance)

- The "www.yourwebsite.com/____" part of the ad.
- It doesn't have to be the actual URL — you can customize it.
- Example: *www.bestlawyer.com/free-consult* feels way more trustworthy than just *www.bestlawyer.com*.
- Tip: Match the path to intent (e.g., /emergency-plumber or /pricing).

Ad Extensions: The Secret Sauce

When I first started, I ignored ad extensions. Big mistake.

Ad extensions don't just make your ad bigger on the page — they add **credibility and click options**.

The most important extensions:

- **Sitelinks** → Direct people to subpages (Pricing, Testimonials, Contact).
- **Call Extensions** → Let people call you directly. Perfect for service

businesses.

- **Location Extensions** → Show your address for local trust.
- **Structured Snippets** → Highlight specific services/products (e.g., "Services: Divorce Law, Family Law, Estate Planning").

Adding these extensions doubled my CTR on one of my campaigns — simply because it made my ad look more trustworthy and clickable compared to competitors.

The 4-Part Formula for High-Converting Ads

Here's the simple structure I use now for all my ads:

Call Out the Intent → Use the keyword in the headline.

- Example: *"Emergency Plumber Near You."*

Promise the Outcome → Show what they'll get.

- Example: *"We Fix Leaks & Burst Pipes Fast."*

Build Credibility → Add proof or trust signals.

- Example: *"24/7 Service. Rated #1 in the City."*

Call to Action (CTA) → Tell them exactly what to do next.

- Example: *"Call Now for Same-Day Service."*

My Big Lesson Here

In the beginning, I wrote ads that were about *me*.

- *"We're the best at what we do."*
- *"We offer professional services."*

But people don't care about us — they care about *themselves.*

The breakthrough came when I started writing ads like I was answering the customer's search:

- They search: *"Best dentist near me."*
- My ad says: *"Top-Rated Dentist Near You — Book Your Appointment Today."*

It feels like a conversation: they ask, and you answer. That's the psychology of a high-converting ad.

Action Steps: Write Your First High-Converting Ad

Pick One Transactional Keyword

- Example: "emergency plumber near me."

Write 3 Headlines

- One with the keyword.
- One with the benefit/outcome.
- One with urgency or credibility.

Write 2 Descriptions

- Use benefits + proof + CTA.
- Example: *"24/7 Plumbers Ready to Help. Same-Day Service Guaranteed. Call Now."*

Add at Least 3 Extensions

- Sitelinks, Call, Location, or Structured Snippets.

Quick Win

- Search your keyword and compare your draft ad to competitors.
- Ask: *If I were the customer, which ad would I click?* If it's not yours, rewrite until it is.

(Expanded with Case Studies): The Anatomy of a High-Converting Search Ad

(content we drafted stays the same up to the Action Steps section — now we insert case studies before the action steps)

Case Study #1: The Local Service Business

A few years ago, I worked with a local plumber who was struggling with Google Ads. His ad looked like this:

Weak Ad (Before):

- Headline: *Plumbing Services Available*
- Description: *We offer affordable plumbing in your area. Call us today.*
- Display Path: *www.plumbercity.com/services*

At first glance, it looks fine, right? But here's the problem:

- It's **generic.** Nothing here screams *emergency help*.
- No credibility or proof.
- No urgency.

Here's the version I rewrote for him:

Strong Ad (After):

- Headline 1: *Emergency Plumber Near You*
- Headline 2: *24/7 Service — Call Now*
- Headline 3: *Leaks & Burst Pipes Fixed Fast*
- Description: *Trusted by 1,200+ Homeowners. Same-Day Repair Guaranteed. Call Today.*
- Display Path: *www.plumbercity.com/emergency*
- Extensions: Call extension + Location + Sitelinks ("Pricing," "Reviews," "Book Online")

The result? His CTR jumped from 1.2% to 5.6% in two weeks — and his cost per lead dropped by 40%. Why? Because this ad matched the customer's **search intent** (urgency + trust).

Case Study #2: The Online Coaching Business

When I first ran ads for my coaching program, I made a rookie mistake: I wrote ads about *me*, not about the client. Here's what I mean:

Weak Ad (Before):

- Headline: *Google Ads Expert Coaching*
- Description: *Learn from my 5+ years of experience. Coaching available online.*
- Display Path: *www.mycoaching.com/googleads*

What's wrong?

- It's all about *me* ("my experience, my coaching").
- It doesn't answer the client's question: *"Can you solve my problem?"*

Here's the ad I rewrote after studying client intent:

Strong Ad (After):

- Headline 1: *Struggling with Google Ads?*
- Headline 2: *Fix Campaigns & Boost ROI Fast*
- Headline 3: *1-on-1 Coaching Available Online*
- Description: *Stop Wasting Ad Spend. Get Proven Strategies Tailored to Your Business. Book Free Call Today.*
- Display Path: *www.mycoaching.com/fix-ads*
- Extensions: Testimonials, FAQ link, Free Call booking page

This simple switch — from "me" to "you" — doubled my conversions. The ad spoke directly to the pain point: wasting money. And it offered a clear next step: book a free call.

Lesson from These Case Studies

The difference between good and bad ads isn't fancy tricks. It's alignment:

- Does your headline match what the customer just searched?
- Does your description speak to their pain and desire?
- Does your display path reassure them they're in the right place?
- Do your extensions make your ad look trustworthy?

Get those right, and your ads stop being ignored and start being clicked.

Action Steps: Write Your First High-Converting Ad

(same as we drafted before — stays here as a natural next step)

The Anatomy of a High-Converting Search Ad

(continuation, after Case Studies section)

Pro Tips: Quick Hacks for Writing Ads That Convert

Here are some of the tricks I've picked up after writing (and rewriting) hundreds of ads:

Use Numbers for Instant Credibility

- Example: *"Trusted by 2,000+ Clients"* or *"Save 30% Today."*
- Numbers break through the noise because they feel specific and real.

Add Urgency Without Sounding Pushy

- Swap *"Call Today"* with *"Same-Day Service"* or *"Limited Spots Available."*
- People act faster when they feel time is limited.

Mirror the Searcher's Words

- If they search *"best dentist near me,"* don't say *"quality dental services."*
- Say *"Top-Rated Dentist Near You."* This small tweak boosts Quality Score.

Test Calls-to-Action (CTAs)

- Don't just settle for *"Call Now."* Try:
- *"Get Free Quote Today"*
- *"Book Your Appointment Online"*

- *"Download Free Guide"* (for coaches/consultants)
- The CTA is often the make-or-break.

Capitalize Smartly for Emphasis

- Example: *"Same-Day Service. Free Estimate. Call Now."*
- Notice how capitalizing each word makes it easier to scan.

Think Like Your Competitor's Customer

- Before running an ad, search your keyword.
- Look at competitor ads.
- Ask: *"What are they missing that I can say better?"*

7

Storytelling with Ad Extensions & Headlines

I used to think Google Ads were just about *keywords*. If I stuffed the keyword into the headline and description, I thought I was doing great. But then I realized something powerful: **ads that tell a story always outperform ads that just state facts.**

Think about it — when someone types a search into Google, they're not just looking for "information." They're in the middle of a story:

- They have a *problem* they want solved.
- They're searching for a *guide* who can solve it.
- They want to know what the *happy ending* looks like.

Your job? Position your ad as the bridge between their problem and their solution. And the best tools to do that on Google are your **headlines and ad extensions.**

Headlines: The 3-Second Storyteller

Headlines aren't just hooks. They're like *chapters* in a micro-story. With 3 available headline slots, you can build a mini narrative:

Headline 1: The Problem / Intent Match

- Directly reflect what they typed.
- Example: *"Emergency Dentist Near You."*

Headline 2: The Promise / Transformation

- Show them what the solution looks like.
- Example: *"Same-Day Relief for Tooth Pain."*

Headline 3: The Proof / Credibility

- Why should they trust you?
- Example: *"Rated #1 Dentist — 1,500+ Happy Patients."*

Together, those headlines tell a story:

- *You're in pain (problem).*
- *We'll solve it fast (solution).*
- *Others trust us too (proof).*

Ad Extensions: The Subplots That Build Trust

When I first started using extensions, I thought of them as "extras." But then I realized — they're actually *supporting characters* in the story. They add credibility, depth, and options.

Here's how to use them strategically:

Sitelink Extensions = Side Doors

- Add links to subpages: Pricing, Reviews, About, Contact.
- Example: A dentist's ad could have sitelinks for *"Insurance Accepted"* and *"Patient Reviews."*
- These give people extra reasons to click — especially if they're not ready to call right away.

Callout Extensions = Bonus Proof Points

- Short phrases like *"Free Consults"* or *"Available 24/7."*
- Think of them as little "story beats" that reinforce your value.

Structured Snippets = Specifics Matter

- Categories like "Services" or "Brands."
- Example: *"Services: Root Canals, Whitening, Implants."*
- These give depth — you're not just a dentist, you're a dentist with *range.*

Call Extensions = The Shortcut Ending

- The best part? With a call button, people don't even need to click your site. They can jump straight to the ending: *calling you right now.*

Location Extensions = Trust through Proximity

- If you're local, this matters. People trust businesses they can *see* on a map.

Case Study: A Simple Story Wins

A client of mine ran ads for their fitness coaching program. At first, their ad looked like this:

Before (Fact-Heavy, No Story):

- Headline: *Fitness Coaching Online*
- Description: *Affordable coaching programs available now. Start today.*

It wasn't bad — but it didn't connect. It felt flat.

We rewrote it to tell a story:

After (Storytelling Headlines + Extensions):

- Headline 1: *Struggling to Lose Weight?*
- Headline 2: *Personalized Coaching That Works*
- Headline 3: *100+ Clients Transformed in 90 Days*
- Description: *Finally break through plateaus. Join our proven system & see results fast.*

Extensions:

- Sitelinks → *"Client Transformations," "Free Consultation," "Pricing Plans."*
- Callouts → *"Custom Meal Plans, Daily Support, Guaranteed Results."*
- Call Extension → Direct number for free consultation.

The difference? The second ad felt like a story:

- The **pain** (struggling to lose weight).
- The **promise** (personalized coaching).
- The **proof** (100+ transformations).
- The **next step** (book now).

That ad got a 3x higher CTR and 2x more conversions.

Pro Tips for Storytelling Headlines & Extensions

- **Think of Headlines as a "Before, After, Bridge"**
- Before: State the pain/problem.
- After: Show the dream outcome.
- Bridge: Why you're the one to deliver it.
- **Rotate Emotional Angles**
- Some ads should emphasize *fear* ("Stop Wasting Ad Spend").
- Others should emphasize *desire* ("Scale Your Business Fast").
- Keep testing — different emotions resonate with different buyers.
- **Don't Waste Extensions**
- Many advertisers add random sitelinks like "Home" or "Blog."
- Instead, use extensions as *objections handlers*: "See Pricing," "Check Reviews," "Book Free Call."

Action Steps: Turn Your Ad into a Story

Pick a Keyword & Write 3 Headlines

- Headline 1 = problem/intent.
- Headline 2 = solution.
- Headline 3 = proof/credibility.

Write 2 Descriptions That Expand the Story

- Show transformation.
- Add urgency + CTA.

Add at Least 3 Extensions That Reinforce the Story

- Sitelinks = subplots.
- Callouts = bonus proof.
- Call/location = fast track to action.

Quick Win

- Search your keyword and read competitor ads.
- Ask yourself: *Do these ads tell a story or just list facts?*
- Then make sure your ad feels like a story that answers the searcher's question better than anyone else's.

Storytelling with Ad Extensions & Headlines

(continuation with bonus section)

Bonus Swipe File: Good vs. Bad Headlines

Here are some real-world headline contrasts I've seen (and tested). Notice how the *bad* versions feel flat, while the *good* ones tell a story or answer intent.

Example 1: Emergency Services
✕ Bad: *Plumbing Services Available*
✐ Good: *Emergency Plumber — 24/7 Fast Repairs*
☞ Why it works: The second headline mirrors urgency, shows availability, and promises speed.

Example 2: Local Business
✕ Bad: *Best Dentist Services*
✐ Good: *Top-Rated Dentist Near You — Book Today*
☞ Why it works: Uses social proof (*top-rated*), relevance (*near you*), and

urgency (*book today*).

Example 3: Coaching/Consulting

× Bad: *Google Ads Coaching Online*

✐ Good: *Struggling with Google Ads? Fix Campaigns Fast*

☞ Why it works: The second version speaks directly to the pain point (*struggling*), then promises a transformation (*fix fast*).

Example 4: E-Commerce

× Bad: *Buy Shoes Online*

✐ Good: *Free Shipping on Running Shoes — Shop Today*

☞ Why it works: Adds a benefit (*free shipping*) and urgency (*shop today*), making it stand out.

Example 5: SaaS / Tech

× Bad: *CRM Software for Businesses*

✐ Good: *Close More Deals with Our CRM — Free Trial Now*

☞ Why it works: Focuses on the *outcome* (closing deals), not just the feature (CRM software).

Takeaway:

Weak headlines are generic, self-focused, or vague. Strong headlines mirror intent, emphasize transformation, and add urgency or credibility.

Action Steps: Turn Your Ad into a Story

(same as written earlier, follows naturally here)

Storytelling with Ad Extensions & Headlines

(continuation with mini exercise worksheet)

Mini Exercise: Headline Upgrade Workshop

Grab a notebook (or open a Google Doc) and practice rewriting headlines. This will train your brain to spot weak ads and instantly make them stronger.

Step 1: Write a Weak Headline (Generic or Self-Focused)

Example: *Affordable Web Design Services*

Step 2: Rewrite It into a Strong Headline (Intent + Benefit + Urgency/Proof)

Example: *Get Your Website Live in 7 Days — Rated #1 in Local Web Design*

✅ **Your Turn:** Write 3 pairs of headlines — one weak, one strong.

- **Pair 1:**
- ✖ Weak: ______________________________
- ✅ Strong: ______________________________
- **Pair 2:**
- ✖ Weak: ______________________________
- ✅ Strong: ______________________________
- **Pair 3:**
- ✖ Weak: ______________________________
- ✅ Strong: ______________________________

Pro Tip: After writing, say the strong headline out loud and imagine you're the customer who just searched for it. Ask: *"Would I click this over the competitor's ad?"* If not, tweak until it feels irresistible.

Action Steps: Turn Your Ad into a Story

(same as before — follows perfectly as a wrap-up)

8

Visual Power — Display & YouTube Ads That Convert

When I first dipped into YouTube and Display campaigns, I treated them like billboards. "Just slap a logo, write 'Best Service in Town,' and people will notice."

They didn't. In fact, my click-through rates were miserable. I wasted thousands testing pretty designs that meant nothing to my audience.

It wasn't until I realized that **visual ads aren't about being pretty — they're about being powerful storytellers in seconds**. When done right, Display and YouTube Ads grab attention, build trust, and drive action — all in under 10 seconds.

The Psychology of Visual Ads

Here's the truth:

- People don't click because your ad looks nice.
- They click because the ad *connects to their story.*

Visual ads need to do 3 things fast:

1. **Stop the Scroll / Grab Attention** (pattern interrupt).
2. **Communicate the Promise** (benefit-focused).
3. **Call for Action** (tell them what to do next).

The Display Ad Framework (Image + Text)

When designing Display Ads (Google's banner ads), think of them as **mini landing pages.**

Key elements:

Headline → Short, bold, benefit-driven.

- Example: *"Fix Google Ads Wasting Money"*

Visual Element → Relevant to the problem or outcome.

- Example: A frustrated business owner (problem) vs. happy business team (outcome).

Branding → Logo small but present (don't make it the hero).

CTA Button → Big, clear, contrasting.

- Examples: *"Book Free Call," "Get Quote," "Watch Demo."*

Rule of thumb: If someone only glances at your display ad for 2 seconds, they should instantly know:

- Who it's for.
- What the benefit is.

- What to do next.

The YouTube Ad Framework (Video)

YouTube is a different beast — but it's my favorite because you can **speak directly** to your Premium Client Avatar.

Think of YouTube Ads as mini-movies, and structure them like this:

Hook (0–5 seconds) → Stop the skip.

- Example: "Are you wasting money on Google Ads and seeing no results?"

Story (5–20 seconds) → Show the pain, then the solution.

- Talk about the frustration your client feels, then position your solution.

Proof (20–40 seconds) → Credibility markers.

- Case studies, results, testimonials, numbers.

Call to Action (40–60 seconds) → Tell them exactly what to do.

- "Click the link below to book your free strategy call."

Pro Tip: Always script for the "skip button." Assume they'll leave in 5 seconds unless you say something so relevant they *must* keep watching.

Case Study: YouTube vs. Display in Action

One of my clients was selling an online fitness program. Here's what happened:

Display Ad (Image):

- Headline: *"Lose Weight Fast — Join Today"*
- Visual: A stock photo of a scale.
- CTA: *"Sign Up Now."*
- Result: 0.9% CTR, very few signups.

YouTube Ad (Video):

- Hook: *"Still trying diet after diet and nothing works?"*
- Story: Coach speaking directly, showing real before/after client photos.
- Proof: *"100+ transformations in the last year."*
- CTA: *"Click the link and start your free 7-day program today."*
- Result: 4.7% CTR, 5x more signups.

Lesson? The **storytelling power** of YouTube crushed the static Display Ad — because it connected emotionally.

Pro Tips: Visual Ads That Work Harder

- **Use Faces** → Ads with real people outperform logos or stock graphics. Humans connect with humans.
- **Add Text Overlay** → On YouTube, add bold text on screen to reinforce your message (for people watching on mute).
- **Show the Transformation** → Before/after visuals are magnetic (struggle → solution).
- **Brand Subtly** → Don't make your logo the star. Make your *message* the star.
- **Design for Mobile First** → Most Display/YouTube traffic is mobile. Text must be readable small.

Bonus Swipe File: Winning CTA Buttons

- *Book Free Call*
- *Get Instant Quote*
- *Start Free Trial*
- *Claim Your Offer Today*
- *Watch Demo Now*

Notice how all of these CTAs are action-driven and specific — no vague "Learn More."

Action Steps: Create Your First Visual Ad Concept

Pick a Core Benefit

- What's the #1 transformation your client avatar wants?

Draft a Display Ad Concept

- Headline + Visual + CTA.
- Keep it simple, bold, and benefit-driven.

Script a 60-Second YouTube Ad

- Hook → Story → Proof → CTA.
- Record it casually with your phone — authenticity beats polish.

Quick Win

- Search YouTube for ads in your niche.
- Watch 3–5 ads and write down:
- What grabbed your attention?
- When did you feel like skipping?

- What CTA made sense?
- Use those notes to improve your own script.

Visual Power — Display & YouTube Ads That Convert

(continuation with mock-up)

🎨 *Visual Mock-Up: Anatomy of a High-Converting Display Ad*

Imagine your ad laid out like a mini billboard. Here's the structure:

```
-----------------------------------------------
|              [Brand Logo - Small]            |
|                                              |
|   Headline: "Fix Google Ads Wasting Money"  |
|                                              |
|   [Image: Frustrated business owner          |
|    looking at laptop + graph going down]     |
|                                              |
|   CTA Button: [ Book Free Call ]             |
 -----------------------------------------------
```

Arrows/Annotations:

- **Logo (Top Corner)** → Keep it visible but not overpowering. Branding should support, not distract.
- **Headline (Bold, Large Font)** → Benefit-driven. Must grab attention in 2 seconds.
- **Image (Center Visual)** → Relatable problem or desired outcome. Avoid cheesy stock images.
- **CTA Button (Bottom)** → Contrasting color, short action phrase like *"Get Quote Today."*

Why this works:

- Headline matches the audience's pain (*wasting money on ads*).
- Visual shows the problem in action (frustration).
- CTA tells them exactly what to do (*book free call*).
- The design is clean — not cluttered with 10 messages.

Pro Tip: If your ad is shrunk down to mobile size, it should *still* be clear at a glance. Test this by zooming your mock-up down to 25% and asking: *Can I still read the headline and CTA?*

Action Steps: Create Your First Visual Ad Concept

(follows naturally from here, as we wrote earlier)

Visual Power — Display & YouTube Ads That Convert

(continuation with YouTube storyboard mock-up)

Storyboard Mock-Up: Anatomy of a High-Converting YouTube Ad

Think of your YouTube ad as a short movie. Here's the structure in text-box format:

```
[HOOK: −05 seconds]
- Speak directly to the problem.
- Example: "Are you tired of wasting money on Google Ads with no
results?"

[STORY: −520 seconds]
- Show the pain point and introduce the solution.
- Example: "I know how frustrating it feels. I was there too,
until I discovered a proven strategy that fixed my campaigns and
doubled my leads."
```

```
[PROOF: -2040 seconds]
- Add credibility, results, or testimonials.
- Example: "Over 500 businesses have used my system, generating
-23x more clients in less than 90 days."

[CALL TO ACTION: -4060 seconds]
- Tell them exactly what to do.
- Example: "Click the link below to book your free strategy call
today and stop wasting ad spend."
```

Why this works:

- The **hook** keeps them from skipping.
- The **story** makes them feel understood.
- The **proof** builds trust.
- The **CTA** drives action while they're most engaged.

Pro Tip: Write your script in short, conversational sentences. Don't read it like a stiff corporate ad — imagine you're talking to a friend over coffee.

Action Steps: Create Your First Visual Ad Concept

(as written earlier, follows naturally)

Visual Power — Display & YouTube Ads That Convert

(continuation with bonus checklist)

Bonus Checklist: 10 Quick Mistakes to Avoid in Display & YouTube Ads

Most advertisers fail not because their budgets are too small — but because they keep repeating the same avoidable mistakes. Here's your no-fluff checklist to stay ahead:

1. **Too Much Text on Display Ads** → Crowded ads get ignored. Stick to *one clear message.*
2. **Weak or Generic Headline** → "Best Service in Town" won't cut it. Always make it benefit-driven.
3. **Stock Images That Scream Fake** → If your image feels staged, trust drops instantly. Use real or relatable visuals.
4. **Logo Overload** → Your brand name shouldn't dominate the ad — the *promise* should.
5. **No CTA Button (or Tiny One)** → People need direction. A bold CTA drives clicks.
6. **Ignoring Mobile Formatting** → Most viewers are on mobile. If text isn't readable small, you're losing.
7. **YouTube Ads That Start Slow** → If your hook doesn't hit in 5 seconds, they'll skip.
8. **Over-Polished, Over-Produced Videos** → Authenticity beats Hollywood-style editing. People trust real over perfect.
9. **No Proof in Video** → Without results, testimonials, or numbers, your ad feels like empty promises.
10. **Vague CTA ("Learn More")** → Always end with a clear next step: *"Book Free Call," "Get Instant Quote," "Start Trial Today."*

Pro Tip: Run through this checklist every time you create a new ad. If you're making 3 Display Ad variations or a new YouTube script, ask: *Am I avoiding all 10 mistakes?* It's a sanity filter that can save you thousands.

Action Steps: Create Your First Visual Ad Concept

(now flows smoothly into the practical exercise we already drafted)

9

Writing Copy That Matches Search Intent

When I first started running Google Ads, I thought copywriting was about being clever. I tried headlines like *"Unlock Your Business Potential Today!"* because it sounded inspirational.

But here's the problem: nobody was typing *"how to unlock my business potential"* into Google. They were searching *"Google Ads agency for dentists"* or *"how to fix high CPC on Google Ads."*

I lost thousands because my copy was talking *at* people, not *with* them.

That's when I learned this truth:

Search ads win when your copy mirrors the exact words, emotions, and urgency of the searcher's intent.

The Three Levels of Search Intent

Think of search intent like a customer's temperature. Your job is to "match the heat."

Cold Intent (Curious but Not Ready)

- Searches: *"What is Google Ads?"* / *"Best ways to get leads online"*
- Copy style: Educational, value-driven.
- Example: *"Learn How Google Ads Can Grow Your Business — Free Starter Guide."*

Warm Intent (Problem-Aware, Exploring Options)

- Searches: *"Google Ads vs Facebook Ads"* / *"How much does Google Ads cost?"*
- Copy style: Comparison, proof-driven.
- Example: *"Cut Costs & Get More Clients with Google Ads — See Proven Results."*

Hot Intent (Buyer-Ready)

- Searches: *"Hire Google Ads expert near me"* / *"Best Google Ads agency for eCommerce."*
- Copy style: Direct, benefit-heavy, CTA-focused.
- Example: *"Google Ads Experts Who Double ROI — Book Free Strategy Call Today."*

Rule of Thumb: Cold → teach. Warm → compare. Hot → sell.

Copywriting Framework: The Mirror Effect

I call this the **Mirror Effect**: your ad copy should feel like a reflection of what the searcher just typed.

- If they typed *"affordable Google Ads agency,"* your headline should say:
- *"Affordable Google Ads Experts — ROI-Driven Campaigns."*
- If they typed *"fix high CPC Google Ads,"* your copy should hit directly:
- *"Cut Your CPC Costs — Proven Google Ads Optimization."*

Don't make them *think* if you're relevant. Make it obvious.

Case Study: Matching vs. Missing Intent

A client once came to me with this ad:

Headline: *"Grow Your Business with Our Award-Winning Agency."*

Search Term Targeted: *"Google Ads expert for eCommerce."*

✗ Result: Low CTR (0.7%), wasted clicks.

We rewrote it to:

Headline: *"eCommerce Google Ads Experts — Scale Sales Fast."*

Description: *"Proven ROI for 150+ eCommerce stores. Book Free Strategy Call Today."*

✅ Result: CTR jumped to 5.2%, cost per lead dropped by 42%.

Lesson? Their original ad was about *them* (award-winning agency). The new ad was about *the searcher's intent* (eCommerce, sales, ROI).

Pro Tips: Writing Copy That Clicks

- **Use Numbers** → Percentages, years of experience, client counts build instant trust.
- **Insert Keywords Naturally** → Don't keyword-stuff, but echo their search.
- **Focus on the "After State"** → Sell the result, not the service. (e.g., *"Get More Patients"* > *"We Run Google Ads"*).
- **Test Power Words** → "Proven," "Fast," "Free," "Exclusive," "Today."
- **Localize When Possible** → "Google Ads Expert in [City]" converts like magic for local intent.

Action Steps: Intent-Matching Copywriting

1. **Pick One Keyword** → Write down a phrase your Premium Client Avatar might search (e.g., *"plumber Google Ads specialist"*).
2. **Write 3 Headlines** that mirror that keyword.
3. **Write 2 Descriptions** — one focused on proof, one on the transformation.
4. **Quick Win**: Search your chosen keyword in Google right now. Look at 3–5 competitor ads. Ask yourself:

Do their headlines match intent?

Are they selling features or outcomes?

How could I beat them?

Writing Copy That Matches Search Intent

(continuation with swipe file)

Bonus Swipe File: Headlines by Intent Level

Here's a ready-made bank of headline examples you can borrow, adapt, and test. Notice how each set mirrors the searcher's *temperature.*

Cold Intent Headlines (educate + attract curiosity)

1. *"New to Google Ads? Free Starter Guide for Local Businesses"*
2. *"Discover How Google Ads Can Bring You Clients"*
3. *"Confused About Online Marketing? See How Google Ads Works"*
4. *"Struggling to Get Leads? Try Google Ads the Right Way"*
5. *"Free Webinar: How Google Ads Grows Small Businesses"*

Goal: Get attention and build awareness, not push for the sale.

Warm Intent Headlines (compare + solve problems)

1. *"Google Ads vs Facebook Ads — What Actually Works?"*
2. *"Cut Costs on Google Ads — Proven Optimization Strategies"*
3. *"See Why 150+ Businesses Switched to Our Google Ads System"*
4. *"Stop Guessing. Start Getting Leads with Google Ads"*
5. *"Affordable Google Ads Experts — Transparent Pricing"*

Goal: Position yourself as the *better* option while solving their concerns.

Hot Intent Headlines (direct + conversion-focused)

1. *"Google Ads Experts for Dentists — Book Free Call Today"*
2. *"eCommerce Google Ads Agency — Double Your Sales Fast"*
3. *"Hire a Certified Google Ads Specialist — ROI Guaranteed"*
4. *"Ready to Scale? Google Ads Campaigns That Convert Now"*
5. *"Stop Wasting Ad Spend — Work With Google Ads Professionals"*

Goal: Remove doubt and give them a clear reason to click *right now*.

How to Use This Swipe File:

- Pick the intent level of your keyword.
- Adapt 2–3 headlines from this list.
- A/B test them to see what resonates.

Action Steps: Intent-Matching Copywriting

(continues seamlessly from here, as drafted earlier)

Writing Copy That Matches Search Intent

(continuation with practice drill)

Mini Practice Drill: Write Headlines That Match Intent

Let's put your new skills into action.

Keyword to Practice With:
"Google Ads agency for real estate agents"
Your Task:

1. Write **one Cold Intent headline** — imagine the searcher is curious, just exploring options.
2. Write **one Warm Intent headline** — they know about Google Ads but want proof, comparisons, or reassurance.
3. Write **one Hot Intent headline** — they're ready to hire or book a call *now*.

Example Answers (for inspiration only):

- Cold: *"How Real Estate Agents Use Google Ads to Get More Listings"*
- Warm: *"Cut Lead Costs — Proven Google Ads Strategies for Realtors"*
- Hot: *"Hire a Google Ads Agency for Realtors — Book Free Call Today"*

Now it's your turn: open a notebook, set a timer for 10 minutes, and write your 3 headlines.

Pro Tip: Read them out loud. If it doesn't sound like something your ideal client would click instantly, tweak it until it does.

10

Keyword Research — Cold, Warm, and High-Intent Keywords

When I first learned about Google Ads, I thought keywords were just about volume. I'd open a keyword tool, see which phrases had the biggest search numbers, and target them all.

The result? My ads showed up everywhere — but for the *wrong people*. People who weren't ready, weren't qualified, or weren't even interested. I burned through budget faster than a rocket.

That's when I learned a lesson I'll never forget:

Keywords aren't about traffic. They're about intent.

If you choose keywords that don't match your client avatar's intent, you're shouting into a crowd of people who will never buy. But when you pick the right intent-driven keywords, your ads become magnets.

The Three Intent Levels of Keywords

Just like in Chapter 8 with ad copy, keywords also live on a spectrum.

1. Cold Intent (Educational & Broad Searches)

- Examples: *"what is Google Ads," "how to get clients online," "marketing for small businesses"*
- Searcher: Curious, not ready to buy.
- Use: Great for building awareness or retargeting lists later.
- Danger: Low conversion, can waste money if used without strategy.

2. Warm Intent (Solution-Seeking Searches)

- Examples: *"Google Ads vs Facebook Ads," "Google Ads pricing," "best PPC strategy"*
- Searcher: Problem-aware, comparing options.
- Use: Excellent for middle-of-funnel ads, nurturing trust.
- Pro Tip: These keywords often lead to cheaper clicks with decent conversion potential.

3. Hot Intent (Buyer-Ready Searches)

- Examples: *"hire Google Ads agency," "Google Ads consultant for dentists," "eCommerce PPC expert"*
- Searcher: Ready to buy or take action.
- Use: Prioritize these first — they're the money-makers.
- Note: High competition, but worth it because ROI is strongest.

The Keyword Pyramid Strategy

Think of your keywords like a pyramid:

```
[Hot Intent] → Fewer searches, high conversion
        [Warm Intent] → Moderate searches, medium conversion
     [Cold Intent] → Broad searches, low conversion
```

The mistake most advertisers make? Spending 80% of their budget at the **bottom** (cold keywords) because it looks like more opportunity.

The smart play? Start at the **top** with hot keywords, layer in warm, and only then sprinkle in cold to build awareness.

Tools I Actually Use (and How I Use Them)

- **Google Keyword Planner** → Free, reliable, straight from Google's database. Great for finding search volume & cost.
- **Ubersuggest / SEMrush / Ahrefs** → Paid tools for deeper competitor keyword spying.
- **Search Term Reports** → Hidden gold. Look at the exact terms triggering your ads. Cut the irrelevant, double down on winners.

Personal Note: I once discovered that a client's ads were showing for "free Google Ads tutorials" — even though they sold premium consulting. No wonder they weren't converting! One look at the Search Term Report saved them thousands.

Case Study: Intent Shift Saves a Campaign

A coaching client of mine was running ads for a fitness app. They targeted:

- *"best weight loss tips," "diet for beginners," "fitness at home."*

CTR was okay, but conversions were dead. Why? These were **cold intent keywords** — people just looking for free advice.

We switched to:

- *"best fitness app for women," "download workout app," "personal trainer online app."*

Result? Conversions doubled in 3 weeks.

Lesson: Always ask: *Is this keyword typed by someone who's curious — or someone who's ready to act?*

Pro Tips: Winning with Keyword Intent

- **Use "Hire" + Industry Keywords** → e.g., *"hire Google Ads expert for dentists"* — always hot intent.
- **Long-Tail Beats Broad** → "Google Ads consultant for real estate" will convert 10x better than just "Google Ads."
- **Negative Keywords Save Money** → Block terms like *"free," "jobs," "tutorial."* They filter out browsers and job seekers.
- **Group by Intent** → Never mix cold, warm, and hot keywords in the same ad group. Your messaging won't match.
- **Start Small, Scale Smart** → Begin with 10–20 laser-focused hot intent keywords. Add more as data rolls in.

Action Steps: Build Your Keyword Intent Map

1. **Choose Your Niche** → Write it down (e.g., dentists, eCommerce, real estate agents).
2. **Brainstorm 10 Hot Intent Keywords** → Use "hire," "expert," "agency," or specific solutions.
3. **Add 10 Warm Intent Keywords** → Use comparisons or problem phrases (e.g., *"Google Ads vs Facebook Ads"*).
4. **Optional: 10 Cold Intent Keywords** → Only if you plan retargeting or awareness campaigns.

5. **Quick Win**: Open your Google Ads account → check your *Search Terms Report* today. Cross out any irrelevant queries and add them as negatives.

Keyword Research — Cold, Warm, and High-Intent Keywords

(continuation with worksheet)

Bonus Worksheet: Build Your Keyword Intent Table

Use this simple table to map out your keywords by intent level. Start with 5–10 phrases for each column.

Cold Intent (Educational) Warm Intent (Comparing Options) Hot Intent (Buyer-Ready)

Cold Intent. Warm Intent (Comparing) Hot Intent (Buyer-Ready)

what is GoogleAds, GoogleAds vs FacebookAds, hire Google Ads expert

best ways to get leads, GoogleAds pricing, GoogleAds agency for dentists

how to market small business, PPC services, eCommerce GoogleAds agency

free marketing strategies, best GoogleAds strategies, certified Google Ads consultant why use online advertising. Google Ads case study. book Google Ads strategy call

How to Use This Table:

1. Fill in with keywords specific to your niche (dentists, eCommerce, real estate, etc.).
2. Highlight your **Top 10 Hot Intent keywords** — these should be your first campaign focus.
3. Save warm and cold intent keywords for retargeting or content-driven campaigns.

Pro Tip: Keep this table alive. As you review your *Search Term Reports*, add new winners and strike out losers. It becomes your personal keyword playbook.

Action Steps: Build Your Keyword Intent Map

(follows naturally from here, as drafted earlier)

Keyword Research — Cold, Warm, and High-Intent Keywords

(continuation with case study exercise)

Case Study Exercise: Classify the Search Terms

A local marketing agency ran ads targeting small business owners. Here are some of the actual search terms that triggered their ads:

1. *"how does Google Ads work"*
2. *"affordable Google Ads agency near me"*
3. *"free Google Ads tutorial"*
4. *"Google Ads vs SEO for leads"*
5. *"hire PPC expert for lawyers"*
6. *"Google Ads certification exam"*
7. *"best PPC company for eCommerce"*

Your task: Classify each keyword as **Cold, Warm, or Hot Intent.**

Answer Key (for reference after they try):

1. *"how does Google Ads work"* → **Cold** (educational).
2. *"affordable Google Ads agency near me"* → **Hot** (buyer-ready).
3. *"free Google Ads tutorial"* → **Cold** (not a paying customer).
4. *"Google Ads vs SEO for leads"* → **Warm** (comparison mode).
5. *"hire PPC expert for lawyers"* → **Hot** (action-ready).
6. *"Google Ads certification exam"* → **Cold** (job seeker/student, irrelevant).
7. *"best PPC company for eCommerce"* → **Hot** (ready to choose a provider).

Lesson: Not every keyword with "Google Ads" in it is valuable. In fact, 2 of these terms (*tutorial, certification*) would drain budget fast because they attract the wrong audience. Meanwhile, the hot-intent terms (*agency, hire, best PPC company*) are gold mines.

Pro Tip: Build the discipline of reviewing **Search Term Reports** weekly. Classify every phrase you see into Cold, Warm, or Hot. Over time, your ad spend will automatically shift toward the most profitable terms.

Action Steps: Build Your Keyword Intent Map

(continues seamlessly from here as we already drafted)

Keyword Research — Cold, Warm, and High-Intent Keywords

(continuation with negative keywords checklist)

Pro Tips Checklist: Negative Keywords That Almost Always Save Money

Here's a list of common negative keywords I add to almost every campaign to filter out bad clicks:

- **"free"** → Attracts browsers, not buyers.
- **"jobs"** / **"careers"** / **"hiring"** → Job seekers, not clients.
- **"training"** / **"course"** / **"tutorial"** → Learners, not customers.
- **"YouTube"** / **"video"** → People looking for free how-to content.
- **"examples"** / **"templates"** → DIY researchers.
- **"certification"** / **"exam"** → Students, not paying clients.
- **"cheap"** → Attracts low-quality leads who usually don't convert.
- **Competitor names** (optional) → Unless you're running a specific competitor campaign, these clicks are usually expensive and unqualified.
- **"review"** / **"rating"** → Early-stage researchers, not ready to buy.

- **"Wikipedia"** / **"definition"** → Purely informational traffic.

Pro Tip: Build your **negative keyword list once**, then apply it across all campaigns. This single step can save 20–30% of wasted ad spend instantly.

Personal Note: I once saved a client $1,200/month by simply adding "free" and "jobs" as negative keywords. They were accidentally paying for clicks from people looking for employment — not leads.

Action Steps: Build Your Keyword Intent Map

(flows into the section we drafted earlier)

11

Retargeting & Similar Audiences with Google's AI

Why Retargeting is the Secret Weapon

Here's a hard truth about online ads: **most people won't convert on their first visit.**

In fact, data shows that up to **97% of website visitors leave without taking action**.

When I first started running Google Ads, I thought every click should turn into a lead. I'd obsessively check the campaign dashboard, wondering why people weren't filling out forms. It wasn't until I embraced *retargeting* that I realized:

People need *multiple touchpoints* before they trust you.

That's where Google's ecosystem becomes incredibly powerful. Unlike many ad platforms, Google lets you follow people across:

- **Search** (text ads)
- **Display** (banners on blogs/news sites)
- **YouTube** (video ads before/during content)
- **Gmail** (sponsored inbox promotions)

So instead of losing a click forever, you get a second, third, or tenth chance to re-engage.

How Retargeting Works (Simple Version)

1. **Tag Visitors** → You add Google's tracking pixel to your site.
2. **Segment the Audience** → Build lists like:

- People who visited your homepage but didn't convert.
- People who checked your pricing page.
- People who watched 50% of your YouTube ad.

1. **Show Follow-Up Ads** → Create ads specifically for these segments.

Example:

- Someone visits your "Google Ads services for dentists" page but leaves.
- Later, they're reading an article on dental marketing.
- Boom — they see your banner ad: *"Still Looking for Google Ads Help? Book a Free Call Today."*

That's the retargeting magic: **right person, right message, right time.**

Similar Audiences: Google's AI Shortcut

Now here's where it gets wild. Google doesn't just help you re-engage lost visitors — it helps you find **new people who behave like them.**

This is called **Similar Audiences** (sometimes called "Lookalike" in other platforms).

Example:

- You upload a list of 1,000 past leads.
- Google's AI analyzes patterns: search behavior, interests, demographics.
- It then finds *tens of thousands* of other people with those same traits.

☞ That's scaling made simple — letting Google do the heavy lifting to discover prospects you never knew existed.

Personal Story: My "Rescue Campaign"

One of my favorite wins came from a client who sold a $3,000 coaching program. We were getting site traffic but very few sign-ups. Instead of panicking, I launched a retargeting campaign with this ad:

"Still thinking it over? Here's a free 15-minute strategy session — no strings attached."

Guess what? Those retargeted clicks converted **4x higher** than cold traffic. In one month, that campaign alone brought in $18,000 in new sales — from people we would've otherwise lost.

☞ Lesson: Don't chase only new clicks. Recycle the ones you already paid for.

Pro Tips for Retargeting Success

- **Segment by behavior** → Don't show the same ad to someone who bounced in 3 seconds vs. someone who viewed your pricing page.
- **Time windows matter** → A 7-day retargeting list is hotter than a 180-day list.
- **Rotate creatives** → People get "ad fatigue" if they see the same banner

20 times.

- **Test softer CTAs** → Instead of hammering "Buy now," try offering free resources, demos, or calls.
- **Cap frequency** → Nobody wants to feel stalked. Limit impressions per user.

Case Study Exercise: Spot the Retargeting Opportunities

Imagine you run a campaign for an **online fitness coaching program.** Your site analytics show:

- 2,000 visitors to the homepage
- 500 visited the "Pricing" page
- 300 started checkout but abandoned
- 200 watched your free webinar but didn't book a call

☞ Question: What retargeting lists would you create?
Example Answers:

- **Homepage visitors** → Show ads about free guides or success stories.
- **Pricing page visitors** → Show testimonials and discount offers.
- **Checkout abandoners** → Show urgency ads ("Spots filling fast, book today").
- **Webinar viewers** → Show reminder ads ("Ready to apply what you learned? Book a strategy call").

Action Steps: Build Your Retargeting Engine

1. Install Google's remarketing tag on your site today.
2. Create at least **3 audience segments** (homepage visitors, pricing visitors, abandoned checkouts).
3. Write one follow-up ad tailored to each segment.
4. Bonus: If you have a client list of 1,000+ emails, upload it to test Similar

Audiences.

(continuation with funnel map)

↯ *Visual Funnel Map: Retargeting in Action*

Think of your Google Ads funnel as a journey from stranger → prospect → client. Retargeting is the "safety net" that catches people who would otherwise slip through.

```
[ COLD TRAFFIC ]↓
    (Search Ads, Display, YouTube)
   People click but don't convert
---------------------------------↓
        Retargeting Kicks In
---------------------------------
[ WARM RETARGETING LISTS ]
   - Homepage visitors
   - Blog readers
   - YouTube viewers↓
    (Show: Free guides, case studies, testimonials)
---------------------------------↓
        Retarget again
---------------------------------
[ HOT RETARGETING LISTS ]
   - Pricing page visitors
   - Checkout abandoners
   - Webinar attendees↓
    (Show: Urgency ads, offers, free calls)
---------------------------------↓
        Conversion
---------------------------------
[ CLIENT ]
   - Booked call
   - Made purchase
   - Signed contract
```

☞ Notice how **cold campaigns feed your retargeting lists**, and those lists drive **warm and hot conversions**. Instead of losing traffic, you recycle it into revenue.

12

Funnel Mapping for Google Ads

Why You Need a Funnel Map

When I first started with Google Ads, I made the same mistake many beginners do:

☞ I treated every campaign like a straight line from **click → sale.**

But here's the truth: Google Ads isn't a straight line. It's a **system of steps** where cold, warm, and hot audiences move through a funnel.

If you don't map this funnel, you'll:

- Overspend on cold traffic.
- Neglect warm leads.
- Miss out on hot buyers who were *this close* to converting.

When I finally sat down and drew my first funnel map, it felt like putting on glasses for the first time. Suddenly, I could see the big picture: not just *ads and clicks*, but **how each campaign connected to revenue.**

The Google Ads Funnel: Cold → Warm → Hot

Let's break it down into three layers:

Cold Traffic (Awareness)

- Who: People who've never heard of you.
- Campaigns: Search ads for broad/educational keywords, YouTube ads, Display awareness.
- Goal: Capture attention, deliver value, build trust.

Warm Traffic (Consideration)

- Who: Visitors who've engaged — checked your services, read a blog, watched your video.
- Campaigns: Retargeting with testimonials, case studies, pricing comparisons.
- Goal: Show proof, remove doubts, keep them moving forward.

Hot Traffic (Conversion)

- Who: Pricing page visitors, checkout abandoners, webinar attendees.
- Campaigns: High-intent keywords, hot retargeting ads.
- Goal: Convert into leads or clients (book a call, make a purchase).

Text-Based Funnel Map

```
[COLD TRAFFIC]↓
    (Search: "what is Google Ads?", YouTube awareness, Display
    ads)
--------------------------------------------------------------
[WARM TRAFFIC]↓
```

```
    Retarget with: case studies, testimonials, pricing comparisons
-------------------------------------------------------------
[HOT TRAFFIC]↓
    Retarget with: urgency ads, free calls, offers
-------------------------------------------------------------
[CONVERSION]→
    Booked Call / Purchase / New Client
```

☞ Notice how each level feeds the next. Cold feeds warm, warm feeds hot, hot feeds conversion.

Personal Story: My First "Full-Funnel" Win

A coaching client of mine once came to me frustrated. They were spending $3,000/month on Google Ads and barely breaking even. Why? They only ran **cold campaigns.**

We mapped their funnel like this:

- **Cold Campaign:** "How to grow your real estate business with ads" (YouTube + Display).
- **Warm Campaign:** Retarget those viewers with "Case Study: Realtor gets 27 leads in 30 days."
- **Hot Campaign:** Retarget pricing page visitors with "Book a Free Strategy Session."

In 60 days, their lead cost dropped by **40%**, and they booked 15 sales calls/month from the same $3,000 budget.

☞ Lesson: Don't just chase clicks. Build **flows**.

Pro Tips for Funnel Mapping

- **Start small**: One cold campaign → one warm retargeting → one hot retargeting is enough to begin.
- **Match content to stage**: Don't pitch hard offers to cold traffic; don't waste case studies on hot checkout abandoners.
- **Track each stage separately**: Use Google Analytics or Ads Manager to see where the leaks are.
- **Automate where possible**: Google's AI can help, but *you* decide the funnel structure.

Mini Exercise: Map Your Funnel

Take one niche or service you're targeting. On a blank page, create three columns:

Cold → Warm → Hot.

1. Write down the keywords, ads, or content you'll use at the **Cold** stage.
2. Write down what retargeting or proof-based ads you'll run at the **Warm** stage.
3. Write down the urgency or conversion ads you'll run at the **Hot** stage.

☞ Example (Dentist Ads):

- Cold: "how to find a new dentist near me" (Search + YouTube awareness ad).
- Warm: Retarget with testimonials from happy patients.
- Hot: Retarget with "Book Your First Appointment — Free Whitening for New Patients."

✅ *Action Steps: Build Your Funnel Map*

1. Draw your **Cold → Warm → Hot funnel** for your current business.
2. Identify at least **one campaign for each stage.**
3. Check if you're overspending on cold clicks and underinvesting in warm/hot.
4. Set a reminder: Review your funnel every 30 days and refine based on results.

By the end of this chapter, readers will stop thinking in **isolated campaigns** and start thinking in **connected systems.** This is the shift from being a campaign manager to being a **client acquisition architect.**

Funnel Mapping for Google Ads

Sample Funnel Templates

Here are three ready-to-use funnel maps you can model. Adapt the details to your niche, but notice how each has the same **Cold → Warm → Hot → Conversion** flow.

1. eCommerce Funnel (Fitness Products Example)

Cold Campaigns

- Search: "best home workout gear"
- YouTube: 30-sec video showing product in action
- Display: Lifestyle banners on health blogs

Warm Campaigns (Retargeting)

- Retarget homepage visitors with: "Why 5,000+ customers love [Brand Name]."
- Retarget product viewers with testimonials or reviews.

Hot Campaigns (Retargeting)

- Cart abandoners: "Your gear is still waiting! Complete checkout today and get free shipping."
- **Conversion**
- Purchase → Upsell email sequence

2. Local Services Funnel (Dentist Example)

Cold Campaigns

- Search: "dentist near me"
- YouTube: Video ad of the clinic with happy patients
- Display: Local news site banners with clinic logo

Warm Campaigns (Retargeting)

- Homepage visitors: "Meet Dr. Smith — 20+ years of trusted dental care."
- Pricing page visitors: "See real patient stories and results."

Hot Campaigns (Retargeting)

- Appointment page visitors: "Book today and get free whitening for new patients."

Conversion

- Book appointment → SMS/Email reminder system

3. Coaching Funnel (Business Coaching Example)

Cold Campaigns

- Search: "how to grow my business online"
- YouTube: Short inspirational ad ("3 steps to double your sales")
- Display: Blog ads on entrepreneurship sites

Warm Campaigns (Retargeting)

- Webinar viewers: "Here's how Sarah doubled her sales with our system."
- Service page visitors: Case study ads or testimonials

Hot Campaigns (Retargeting)

- Webinar attendees who didn't book: "Ready to take the leap? Free strategy session this week only."
- Pricing page visitors: "Spots are limited — secure your coaching call today."

Conversion

- Book strategy call → Enroll in coaching program

Takeaway:

The funnel structure doesn't change much across niches. What changes is the **messaging** and **offer**. Whether you're selling dumbbells, dental appointments, or coaching calls — the Cold → Warm → Hot journey stays the same.

✅ *Action Steps: Build Your Funnel Map*

(flows naturally into the section we already drafted)

Funnel Mapping for Google Ads

(continuation with mistakes checklist)

⚠️ *Funnel Mistakes to Avoid*

Even the smartest campaigns fail if the funnel is broken. Watch out for these common traps:

1. **Only running cold campaigns** → You'll pay for clicks that never convert without retargeting.
2. **Using the same ad for all audiences** → Cold, warm, and hot prospects need different messages.
3. **Forgetting the follow-up** → Don't let conversions end at the ad. Pair your funnel with email/SMS nurture.
4. **Overspending on cold traffic** → Allocate more budget to warm/hot where ROI is highest.
5. **No clear CTA at each stage** → Awareness ads should educate, not sell. Hot ads should drive immediate action.
6. **Ignoring tracking/analytics** → If you don't measure funnel stages separately, you won't know where the leaks are.
7. **Neglecting creative refreshes** → Old ads cause ad fatigue and kill retargeting performance.
8. **Overcomplicating funnels too soon** → Start simple (1 cold, 1 warm, 1 hot). Build complexity later.

9. **Not excluding existing buyers** → Wasting ad spend showing conversion ads to people who already purchased.
10. **Treating funnels as "set and forget"** → Funnels evolve. Review and optimize every 30–60 days.

Pro Tip: A funnel isn't about perfection on day one. It's about iteration. Launch simple, test, and refine.

Funnel Mapping for Google Ads

(final enrichment with audit exercise)

Mini Audit Exercise: Classify Your Current Campaigns

Grab a notebook, Google Sheet, or even a whiteboard. Let's quickly audit your current campaigns.

Step 1: List all active campaigns.

- Write down each campaign name (e.g., "Search – Dentist Near Me," "YouTube – Free Training," "Display – Retarget Visitors").

Step 2: Assign each campaign to a funnel stage.

- **Cold Traffic** → Campaigns targeting broad keywords, awareness ads, YouTube reach.
- **Warm Traffic** → Retargeting ads, proof-driven campaigns (case studies, testimonials).
- **Hot Traffic** → Retargeting checkout/cart visitors, high-intent search ("buy," "book," "near me").

Step 3: Spot the gaps.

- Do you have campaigns in *all three* stages?

- Are you overspending on cold while neglecting warm/hot?
- Are you running too many warm/hot ads without enough cold leads to feed them?

Step 4: Adjust priorities.

- Circle the funnel stage you're strongest in.
- Star the funnel stage you're weakest in (that's your next area of focus).

✅ **Quick Win:** By the time you finish this 15-minute audit, you'll see whether you're running a *real funnel* or just a set of disconnected campaigns. This clarity alone can save you thousands in wasted ad spend.

Remember: Funnels aren't about running "more campaigns." They're about running the **right campaigns in the right sequence.**

Funnel Mapping for Google Ads

(final touch — preview into Chapter 12)

Preview: Budget Leak Warning Signs

Before we dive into Chapter 12, let me give you a quick taste of what's coming. Even a perfectly mapped funnel can **bleed money** if you're not careful.

Here are the **early warning signs** your funnel is draining your budget:

- **High spend, low conversions** → If you're pumping money into cold traffic with no warm/hot follow-up.
- **Sky-high CPC (Cost Per Click)** → You're bidding blindly or letting Google overspend on weak keywords.

- **Retargeting running too long** → Showing the same ad for months, annoying prospects instead of converting them.
- **Unbalanced spend** → 80% cold, 20% warm/hot. (Hint: this ratio is usually upside down.)
- **Paying for irrelevant clicks** → Missing negative keywords or poor targeting filters.

If you catch one or more of these leaks in your audit, don't panic — we'll fix them in the next chapter.

13

Budgeting & Bidding Strategies

Why Budgeting & Bidding Make or Break Your Funnel

When I first ran Google Ads, I thought the secret was in the ads themselves — the copy, the keywords, the visuals. And yes, that matters. But here's what nobody told me at the start:

Even the best ad fails with the wrong budget and bidding strategy.

I've seen businesses waste thousands because they either:

- Spent 90% of their budget on cold traffic and had nothing left to retarget.
- Chose automated bidding before Google had enough data to optimize.
- Set a "peanut budget" that spread too thin across too many campaigns.

Budgeting and bidding are like **fuel and gears** in a race car. You need enough fuel (budget) in the right tank (funnel stage), and you need the right gear (bidding) for the track you're on.

The 70/20/10 Rule for Funnel Budgets

Here's a simple starting framework for distributing your ad spend:

70% Cold Traffic (Awareness)

- Search ads for broad or educational intent
- YouTube or Display awareness campaigns
- Purpose: Fill the top of the funnel with new eyes

20% Warm Traffic (Consideration)

- Retargeting visitors who've engaged with your site, YouTube, or Display
- Purpose: Nurture trust with testimonials, proof, and offers

10% Hot Traffic (Conversion)

- High-intent keywords ("buy," "near me")
- Retargeting checkout/cart abandoners or pricing page visitors
- Purpose: Drive immediate conversions

Over time, you'll often **flip this ratio** as warm/hot traffic grows more valuable. But start with 70/20/10 so your funnel doesn't starve at the top.

Daily Budget Rule of Thumb

- **Cold Campaigns**: Start with at least \$20–\$50/day per campaign to gather meaningful data.
- **Warm Retargeting**: \$10–\$30/day depending on site traffic.
- **Hot Retargeting**: \$5–\$15/day is often enough (small, high-intent audience).

Remember: Google needs data. Running \$5/day across 10 campaigns gives you *"peanuts data" — which means no optimization. Better to run 1–2 campaigns with solid daily budgets than 10 starving campaigns.*

Bidding Strategies Simplified

Google Ads gives you a buffet of bidding options. Here's how I think about them:

Manual CPC (Cost Per Click)

- Best for beginners who want maximum control.
- You set the bids per keyword.
- Downside: Slower scaling, requires babysitting.

Maximize Clicks

- Google tries to get as many clicks as possible within your budget.
- Works if your goal is traffic, but not great for conversions.

Maximize Conversions (Smart Bidding)

- Google auto-adjusts bids to get conversions within budget.
- Best once you have **at least 30–50 conversions** in the last 30 days (so Google has data).

Target CPA (Cost Per Acquisition)

- You tell Google "I want leads at $X cost," and it adjusts bids to hit that goal.
- Works beautifully once you know your real target CPA.

Target ROAS (Return on Ad Spend)

- You tell Google "I want $3 back for every $1 spent."
- Best for eCommerce or businesses with clear purchase values.

☞ My rule: **Start manual → graduate to smart bidding once you have enough data.**

Personal Story: The $500/Day Rookie Mistake

A client once called me in a panic: "We're spending $500 a day and nothing's working!"

When I checked, I saw they were running **Maximize Conversions** with *zero historical data*. Google was guessing — and guesswork at $500/day is an expensive game.

We dialed back to **Manual CPC** for 30 days, gathered data, then switched to **Target CPA** once we had 40+ conversions. Their cost per lead dropped from $90 to $32.

☞ Lesson: Don't hand over the steering wheel to Google until it knows how to drive your car.

Pro Tips for Budgeting & Bidding

- **Start with a test budget**: 2–3x your target CPA per day is a good benchmark (if you want $50 leads, spend ~$100–$150/day).
- **Segment budgets by funnel stage**: Don't let cold traffic hog money meant for warm/hot conversions.
- **Watch for "Budget Limited" warnings**: If you're capped too early in the day, raise budget or tighten targeting.
- **Scale winners, not losers**: Double down on campaigns that prove ROI before adding more spend.

- **Review weekly, optimize monthly**: Daily tweaks cause chaos; give Google time to learn.

Mini Exercise: Build Your Budget Plan

On a piece of paper (or spreadsheet), sketch this out:

Your total monthly ad budget.

- Example: $3,000/month.

Split by funnel stage using 70/20/10.

- Cold: $2,100/month ($70/day)
- Warm: $600/month ($20/day)
- Hot: $300/month ($10/day)

Pick your bidding strategy.

- Cold: Manual CPC (control spend, gather data).
- Warm: Maximize Clicks or Manual CPC (small audiences).
- Hot: Target CPA (once you know your numbers).

Set a review date.

1. Every 30 days, review results and shift budgets based on ROI.

✅ Action Steps

1. Write down your **total ad budget** for the next 30 days.
2. Apply the **70/20/10 split** across Cold → Warm → Hot campaigns.
3. Choose your **bidding strategy** for each stage (start manual, move to smart bidding later).

4. Set a calendar reminder to **review spend allocation** in 30 days.

By the end of this chapter, readers stop "guessing" at ad spend and start funding their funnel like an investor — with strategy, structure, and control.

Budget Leak Checklist

Here are the most common ways advertisers unknowingly pour money down the drain:

Overspending on Cold Traffic

- 90% of your budget goes to awareness ads, with nothing left to retarget warm/hot audiences.

Too Many Campaigns, Too Little Budget

- Running 8–10 campaigns at $5/day each → not enough data for optimization.

Skipping Negative Keywords

- Paying for clicks like "free," "jobs," or "cheap" that will never convert.

Letting Google Run Fully Automated Bidding Too Soon

- Switching to Target CPA/ROAS with *no historical data* → Google guesses with your wallet.

Budget Limited Campaigns

- Ads cut off by noon because your daily cap is too low → lost conversions.

Ignoring Seasonality

- Keeping budgets flat year-round, even when demand spikes (holidays, tax season, back-to-school).

Retargeting Overkill

- Showing the same retargeting ad 20 times → prospects tune out or block you.

No Warm/Hot Layer

- Running cold ads only and wondering why nobody buys.

Not Segmenting Branded vs. Non-Branded Campaigns

- Paying top dollar to bid on your own business name when you could dominate it cheaper.

Set-and-Forget Mentality

- Leaving budgets untouched for months without checking ROI → silent leaks.

Pro Tip: Each month, run your budget through this checklist. Even fixing one leak can free up 10–20% of wasted ad spend.

Budgeting & Bidding Strategies

(mini case study addition)

Mini Case Study: Plugging a $2,000/Month Leak

One of my coaching clients, a local HVAC company, came to me frustrated:

"We're spending $4,000 a month on Google Ads... and barely getting calls."
When I looked under the hood, here's what I found:

- **90% of their budget** was going to cold traffic campaigns.
- They had **zero retargeting** for warm visitors who had already checked their site.
- Worst of all, they were paying for irrelevant clicks like "HVAC jobs" and "free air conditioning repair" because they had no **negative keywords** set.

That meant about $2,000/month was being wasted.
Here's what we did in 30 days:

1. Reallocated spend using the **70/20/10 rule** (Cold/Warm/Hot).
2. Added a simple **retargeting campaign** to follow site visitors with an ad offering "$50 off first repair call."
3. Built a **negative keyword list** ("jobs," "free," "DIY," "training").

Results:

- Lead cost dropped from **$120 → $48.**
- Calls increased by **3x** in the first 6 weeks.
- They saved **$2,000/month** that was previously being burned on irrelevant clicks.

☞ Lesson: You don't always need to spend *more* — you often just need to spend *smarter.*

Think of budgeting like plumbing. If the pipes are leaking, adding more water (money) won't help. Fix the leaks, then turn up the pressure.

Budgeting & Bidding Strategies

(final touch)

Preview: Data Tracking Prep

Now that you've built a smart budget and plugged the leaks, here's the truth:
☞ **A budget only works if you can read the data.**
Without tracking:

- You won't know which campaigns are profitable vs. which are money pits.
- You'll guess whether your $50/day is actually creating ROI.
- You'll either overspend out of fear… or underspend out of confusion.

Before we move into optimization, ask yourself:

- Do I have **conversion tracking** set up for leads, calls, or purchases?
- Can I see **CTR (Click-Through Rate), Quality Score, and ROAS** in my account?
- Am I reviewing performance by **funnel stage** (cold, warm, hot) instead of lumping all results together?

We'll decode these numbers so you can read your Google Ads dashboard like a pro investor scanning a stock portfolio.

Core Metrics to Emphasize (Basic Must-Knows)

These are the **non-negotiables** every reader should understand:

1. **CTR (Click-Through Rate)** → Are your ads grabbing attention?
2. **Quality Score** → How Google judges your ads (relevance, CTR, landing page experience).
3. **CPC (Cost Per Click)** → How much you're paying for each click.
4. **Conversion Rate** → What % of clicks turn into leads/sales.
5. **CPA (Cost Per Acquisition)** → The real price of each lead/client.

Level 2 Metrics (Intermediate / Advanced)

These add depth once the basics are covered:

6. **Impression Share** → How often your ads show up vs. competitors.
7. **ROAS (Return on Ad Spend)** → Revenue generated per $1 spent.
8. **View-Through Conversions (VTC)** → Especially for Display & YouTube.
9. **Attribution Models** → First-click vs. last-click vs. data-driven.

Mentor-Level Insights (Pro Tips)

This is where your personal touch can shine, showing readers what *really* matters long-term:

- Don't obsess over CTR if CPA is healthy.
- Quality Score is a lever for cheaper clicks — fix relevance first.
- ROAS can mislead if you ignore **customer lifetime value (CLV).**
- Always track by **funnel stage** (Cold/Warm/Hot), not just overall account averages.

14

Reading the Data — CTR, Quality Score, ROAS

From Dashboard Confusion to Data Confidence

When I first logged into my Google Ads dashboard, it felt like staring at the cockpit of a plane. Numbers everywhere. Acronyms I didn't understand. Metrics flashing red or green.

☞ I made the rookie mistake of tracking *everything*.

And when you track everything, you actually track nothing.

It wasn't until I focused on a handful of **key metrics** that things clicked. These were the numbers that actually told me if I was making money… or burning it.

The 5 Metrics That Matter Most

Let's keep this simple. If you understand these five, you can already outsmart 90% of advertisers.

CTR (Click-Through Rate)

- **What it means:** The percentage of people who saw your ad and clicked.
- **Why it matters:** Low CTR = your ad isn't resonating. High CTR = your message matches intent.
- **Good benchmark:** 3–5% for Search campaigns is solid.

Quality Score

- **What it means:** Google's 1–10 rating of your ad's relevance (ad copy, keyword, landing page).
- **Why it matters:** Higher Quality Score = cheaper clicks. Lower Quality Score = Google makes you pay a tax.
- **Good benchmark:** Aim for 7/10 or higher.

CPC (Cost Per Click)

- **What it means:** How much you're paying for each click.
- **Why it matters:** High CPC is fine if those clicks turn into clients. Low CPC is useless if it's junk traffic.
- **Good benchmark:** Depends on niche. Focus less on "cheap clicks," more on "profitable clicks."

Conversion Rate (CVR)

- **What it means:** The % of visitors who take action (form fill, purchase, call).
- **Why it matters:** This is where the magic happens. A 10% landing page

beats a 2% one every time.
- **Good benchmark:** 5–10% is strong for lead gen.

CPA (Cost Per Acquisition/Lead)

- **What it means:** The real cost of a lead or sale.
- **Why it matters:** This is the bottom line. If it's lower than your target, you're winning. If not, something's broken.
- **Good benchmark:** Depends on your profit margins. Always know your break-even CPA.

Light Touch: The Next-Level Metrics

Once you've mastered the basics, here are two advanced metrics to keep an eye on (but don't obsess over yet):

- **Impression Share** → How often your ads show vs. competitors. If you're under 50%, competitors are eating your lunch.
- **ROAS (Return on Ad Spend)** → Revenue per $1 spent. Great for eCommerce, but only meaningful if you track sales properly.

☞ For now, keep these in your back pocket. Focus on CTR, Quality Score, CPC, Conversion Rate, and CPA first.

Personal Story: The CTR Trap

I once worked with a client who was *obsessed* with CTR. "Our CTR is 10%! We're crushing it!"

But when I looked deeper, their CPA was sky-high. They were getting cheap clicks on curiosity-driven ads that didn't convert.

☞ Lesson: Don't let a single shiny metric blind you. Always pair **CTR** with **CPA.**

Mini Exercise: Your Data Snapshot

Open your Google Ads dashboard right now. Write down these five numbers for your main campaign:

- CTR = ____ %
- Quality Score = ____ /10
- CPC = $ ____
- Conversion Rate = ____ %
- CPA = $ ____

Now answer:

1. Which number looks strongest?
2. Which number looks weakest?
3. If you had to improve just *one metric* next month, which one would move the needle most?

✅ *Action Steps*

1. **Track the Big 5** (CTR, Quality Score, CPC, Conversion Rate, CPA) weekly.
2. **Don't obsess over averages** — always segment by campaign or funnel stage.
3. **Pick one metric per month to improve** (e.g., "this month we're lowering CPA").
4. **Ignore vanity metrics** (impressions, clicks) unless they tie to conversions.

Reading the Data — CTR, Quality Score, ROAS

Metrics Cheat Sheet (Screenshot This!)

- **CTR (Click-Through Rate):** % of people who saw your ad and clicked.
- **Quality Score:** Google's 1–10 rating of ad + keyword + landing page relevance.
- **CPC (Cost Per Click):** How much you pay for each click.
- **Conversion Rate (CVR):** % of visitors who complete your goal (lead, sale, call).
- **CPA (Cost Per Acquisition):** Cost to acquire a lead or customer.
- **Impression Share:** % of eligible times your ad appeared vs. competitors.
- **ROAS (Return on Ad Spend):** Revenue earned per $1 spent on ads.

☞ *Tip: Focus on the top 5. The others are "bonus" metrics once you're comfortable with the basics.*

A/B Testing Framework Options

1. Beginner-Friendly (Simple Split Tests) — ✓ I'd emphasize this most

- **What it is:** Test *one variable at a time* (e.g., headline A vs. headline B).
- **Why:** Keeps things simple, gives clean results, and builds confidence.
- **Examples to test first:**
- Headlines (different promises, benefits, or CTAs).
- Landing page CTAs ("Get Your Free Quote" vs. "Start Today").
- Ad descriptions (emotional vs. logical).

☞ This is where 80% of readers should start.

2. Intermediate (Ad Group Split Testing)

- **What it is:** Run multiple ads in one ad group and let Google optimize.
- **Why:** Efficient way to see what message resonates without micromanaging.
- **Examples:** 3 headline combos inside one ad group → monitor CTR + CPA.

3. Advanced (Multivariate Testing) — just a light touch mention

- **What it is:** Testing multiple variables at once (e.g., headline, CTA, and image).
- **Why:** Useful for high-budget advertisers or agencies.
- **Risk:** Requires more traffic and data, otherwise results are muddy.

15

A/B Testing Headlines, Ads & Landing Pages

When I first started running Google Ads, I thought I was a genius copywriter. Every headline I wrote felt like a masterpiece. But here's the truth: **what I *thought* would win often lost — badly.**

One time, I wrote a clever headline I was sure would crush it. Turns out, the "boring" one with a simple benefit ("Save 30% on Same-Day Plumbing") got triple the clicks.

☞ Lesson: Don't guess. **Test.**

The Power of Simple A/B Testing

A/B testing is just a fancy way of saying:

- Run **Version A** vs. **Version B**.
- Change **one variable at a time.**
- See which one performs better.

That's it. You don't need a PhD in statistics.

Why it works:

- Strips away guesswork.
- Gives you hard data on what your Premium Client Avatar responds to.
- Builds confidence in your marketing decisions.

What to Test First

Don't try to test everything at once. Start with the big levers:

Headlines (Ad Level)

- Example: "24/7 Emergency Locksmith" vs. "Locked Out? Get Back Inside Fast."
- Metric to watch: **CTR (Click-Through Rate).**

Descriptions (Ad Level)

- Example: Emotional vs. logical copy.
- Metric to watch: **CTR + Conversion Rate.**

Landing Page Call-to-Action (CTA)

- Example: "Book Your Free Consultation" vs. "Get Your Quote Now."
- Metric to watch: **Conversion Rate.**

Form Layout (Landing Page)

- Example: Short form (name + email) vs. longer form (with phone number).
- Metric to watch: **Conversion Rate + Lead Quality.**

Side Notes: Intermediate & Advanced

- **Intermediate:** Let Google rotate multiple ads within an ad group (great way to test 3–4 variations at once).
- **Advanced:** Multivariate testing (changing multiple elements simultaneously). Useful for high-budget accounts, but messy if you don't have tons of data.

☞ For now? Stick with simple A/B testing until you're seeing at least **100+ clicks per variation.**

Pro Tips Box: Testing Do's & Don'ts

✅ **Do** test one thing at a time.
✅ **Do** give your test enough data (at least a few hundred impressions or 50+ clicks).
✅ **Do** let the data run — don't kill a test after one day.
× **Don't** declare a winner too early.
× **Don't** test random things that don't impact conversions.
× **Don't** forget to apply your learnings across campaigns.

Mini Exercise: Your First A/B Test

This week, pick ONE thing to test. Write it here:

- Test element: ____________
- Version A: ____________
- Version B: ____________

Set it up in Google Ads, run it for 1–2 weeks, and record the results.

✅ *Action Steps*

1. Choose one ad or landing page element to test this week.
2. Run a simple A/B test with two variations.
3. Measure results using the right metric (CTR, Conversion Rate, CPA).
4. Keep a "Testing Journal" — every test teaches you something about your audience.

A/B Testing Headlines, Ads & Landing Pages

Bonus: Testing Ideas Swipe File (10 Prompts to Try)

Not sure what to test first? Use these 10 ready-to-go testing prompts.

Headline Angle:

- A: "24/7 Emergency Plumbing"
- B: "Same-Day Plumbing — Save 30% Today"

CTA Language:

- A: "Get a Free Quote"
- B: "Book Your Consultation Now"

Emotional vs. Logical Copy:

- A: "Never Miss Another Deadline"
- B: "Project Management That Saves 10 Hours a Week"

Benefit Order:

- A: Lead with speed ("Fast Results")
- B: Lead with savings ("Cut Costs")

Display Path in URL:

- A: www.example.com/**free-trial**
- B: www.example.com/**get-started**

Form Fields:

- A: Short form (Name + Email)
- B: Longer form (Name, Email, Phone)

Ad Extensions:

- A: Add call extension
- B: Add sitelinks to services

Headline Numbers:

- A: "Trusted by 500+ Clients"
- B: "Over $2M in Sales Generated"

Landing Page CTA Placement:

- A: CTA button above the fold
- B: CTA button after benefits section

Offer Framing:

- A: "Free Consultation"
- B: "$100 Value Consultation — Yours Free"

☞ Use these prompts to spark ideas, but remember: always test ONE thing at a time.

Scaling Approaches We Could Emphasize

1. Beginner-Level Overview (Recommended for Most Readers)

- **Smart Campaigns** = Google automates targeting, bidding, and ad creation.
- Pros: Easy to set up, less to manage, good for small budgets.
- Cons: Less control, "black box" decision-making, sometimes wastes money.
- **Manual Campaigns** = You control keywords, bids, targeting.
- Pros: More control, transparency, better for scaling.
- Cons: Steeper learning curve, more setup.
- Focus on **when to use Smart vs. Manual** (based on budget size, experience, goals).

☞ This approach helps beginners avoid overwhelm while still planting the seed that control matters at scale.

2. Intermediate (Balanced Approach)

- Compare **Smart Bidding strategies** (Maximize Clicks, Target CPA, Target ROAS).
- Show **when to switch from Manual CPC → Automated bidding.**
- Examples of hybrid setups (manual campaign structure + smart bidding).
- Use of **Performance Max campaigns** (pros, cons, niches it works for).

3. Advanced (Agency/Pro Level)

- Deep dive into **Performance Max vs. Standard Shopping** for eCom.
- Discuss **automation layering** (manual audience segmentation + smart bidding).
- Show how to scale campaigns with **scripts, rules, and API integrations.**
- Case study of scaling from $1k → $50k/month using automation.

16

Scaling with Smart Campaigns vs. Manual Control

My Early Scaling Mistake

When I first tried to scale my ads, I leaned hard on Google's **Smart Campaigns.** It felt easy — like letting the autopilot fly the plane.

For a while, the results were okay. But then I noticed something troubling: I was spending more… and getting less. Leads were random, costs were unpredictable, and I didn't know why.

That's when I realized: **Smart Campaigns are like training wheels. Helpful when you're new, but dangerous when you're trying to win the race.**

Smart Campaigns: The Training Wheels

What They Are:

Google sets everything up for you — keywords, bidding, targeting, even ad variations.

Pros:

- Easy setup (few clicks and you're live).
- Good for local businesses with tiny budgets.
- Low time commitment.

Cons:

- Limited control (Google decides what's "best").
- Wasted budget (ads may show to irrelevant audiences).
- Harder to track what's actually working.

☞ Bottom line: **Smart Campaigns are fine for beginners testing the waters — not for serious scaling.**

Manual Control: The Driver's Seat

What It Is:

You choose your keywords, targeting, bidding, and ad formats.

Pros:

- Full control over where your money goes.
- Transparency (you see what's working, what's not).
- Ability to scale predictably.

Cons:

- Steeper learning curve.
- Takes more time and attention.

☞ Bottom line: **Manual campaigns let you grow strategically, not blindly.**

Light Touch: Smart Bidding

Within manual campaigns, Google offers **Smart Bidding strategies** (this is where automation *can* help if used correctly):

- **Maximize Clicks** → Great for early testing.
- **Target CPA (Cost Per Acquisition)** → Google tries to hit your cost-per-lead goal.
- **Target ROAS (Return on Ad Spend)** → Google optimizes for revenue vs. cost (best for eCommerce).

My advice: Start with **Manual CPC or Maximize Clicks**. Once you have 20–30 conversions, experiment with **Target CPA.**

Pro Tips Box: Scaling the Smart Way

✅ Don't double your budget overnight — increase by 20–30% at a time.
✅ Always scale what's *already working* (don't pour money into broken ads).
✅ Use Smart Bidding *after* you've collected enough conversion data.
✕ Don't rely on Smart Campaigns for long-term scaling.

Mini Exercise: Your Scaling Plan

Write down your current main campaign:

- Campaign type: Smart / Manual?
- Daily budget: $ ____

- CPA goal: $ ____

Now answer:

1. Is this campaign ready for manual control?
2. Could I increase budget by 20–30% without breaking ROI?
3. Do I have enough conversions to test a smart bidding strategy?

✅ Action Steps

1. Review your current campaigns. If you're using **Smart Campaigns**, consider moving your best one into **Manual** for more control.
2. Pick a **single campaign** to scale by 20–30% this month.
3. Track results using your **Big 5 metrics** (CTR, Quality Score, CPC, Conversion Rate, CPA).
4. Experiment with **Target CPA bidding** once you've hit 20–30 conversions.

👉 With this chapter, readers learn the **difference between letting Google run the show vs. taking the wheel.** And they'll see scaling as a step-by-step process — not a gamble.

Scaling Pitfalls Checklist

Before you scale your budget, avoid these 5 classic mistakes:

Scaling a Broken Campaign

- If your ads aren't profitable at $20/day, they won't magically become profitable at $200/day. Fix first, then scale.

Doubling Budgets Overnight

- Sudden jumps confuse Google's algorithm. Increase by 20–30% max at a time.

Chasing Cheap Clicks

- More traffic isn't better traffic. Focus on conversion cost, not CPC.

Ignoring Conversion Data

- If you don't have at least 20–30 conversions, smart bidding strategies won't optimize properly.

Scaling Too Many Campaigns at Once

- Pick one winning campaign to scale. Scatter your focus and you'll dilute results.

☞ Print this list or keep it on your desk. Scaling is exciting, but discipline beats impatience every time.

1. Beginner Errors (Setup & Basics)

These are the rookie mistakes that waste money fast:

- Using **broad match keywords** without negatives.
- Sending all traffic to the homepage (instead of a landing page).
- Not setting up **conversion tracking** (flying blind).
- Writing ads for themselves instead of their **Premium Client Avatar**.

☞ These resonate with new readers (and make them feel "I've been there too").

2. Strategy Errors (Scaling & Targeting)

These are mid-level mistakes that hurt ROI:

- Scaling too early (before proving ROI).
- Testing too many variables at once.
- Over-relying on **Smart Campaigns**.
- Ignoring the funnel (treating cold, warm, hot traffic the same).

☞ Perfect link from Chapter 15 into more strategic thinking.

3. Compliance Issues (Google Policy Traps)

These are mistakes that can get accounts suspended:

- Using restricted words (like “best,” “guaranteed,” “cure”).
- Violating ad policies (misleading claims, lack of disclaimers).
- Not respecting privacy/tracking rules (GDPR, cookie consent, etc.).
- Copying competitors’ ad text too closely.

☞ Advanced readers will appreciate this, and beginners will feel safer knowing the rules.

4. Optimization Errors (Data & Testing)

These are about failing to refine:

- Killing tests too early.
- Obsessing over CTR but ignoring CPA.
- Not segmenting by device, time, or location.
- Letting Google spend on irrelevant placements (Display/YouTube).

☞ This ties into the **A/B testing & data chapters** for consistency.

17

Common Mistakes in Google Ads

My $2,000 Mistake (So You Don't Make It Too)

I'll never forget the time I launched a campaign, forgot to set negative keywords, and woke up the next morning to see half my budget gone — on irrelevant searches that had nothing to do with my offer.

☞ That mistake cost me over $2,000 before I caught it. Painful? Yes.

But it taught me something priceless: **the fastest way to win with Google Ads is to avoid the most common mistakes.**

1. Beginner Errors (Setup & Basics)

These are the rookie traps most advertisers fall into when they're just starting out:

- **Broad Match Overload** → Running only broad match keywords without negatives. This pulls in irrelevant searches (and drains budget fast).
- **Sending Traffic to the Homepage** → Your homepage is not a sales page. Always direct clicks to a **dedicated landing page** that matches the ad.

- **No Conversion Tracking** → If you don't track conversions, you're flying blind. You'll never know what's working.
- **Writing Ads for Yourself, Not Clients** → Ads that sound clever to you often flop. Always write for your **Premium Client Avatar.**

2. Strategy Errors (Scaling & Targeting)

Even experienced advertisers slip here:

- **Scaling Too Early** → If it doesn't work at $20/day, it won't work at $200/day.
- **Testing Too Many Variables at Once** → Changing headlines, CTAs, and images all at the same time means you'll never know what actually worked.
- **Over-Relying on Smart Campaigns** → Great for testing, dangerous for scaling.
- **Ignoring the Funnel** → Treating cold, warm, and hot traffic the same is like proposing marriage on the first date.

3. Compliance Issues (Google Policy Traps)

This is the sneaky category that can get your account suspended overnight:

- **Using Restricted Words** → Words like "best," "guaranteed," or health-related claims (like "cure" or "instant fix") are red flags.
- **Misleading Claims** → If your ad promises one thing but your landing page delivers another, you risk suspension.
- **Privacy Violations** → Not disclosing how you collect data, or ignoring GDPR/cookie policies.
- **Copying Competitors** → Google flags duplicate ad text — and you don't want legal trouble either.

☞ I once had a client's campaign paused for a single word in the headline.

Don't play fast and loose with compliance.

4. Optimization Errors (Data & Testing)

These are the mistakes that quietly drain money over time:

- **Killing Tests Too Early** → Declaring winners after just a day or two. Data needs time.
- **Chasing CTR Instead of CPA** → A flashy ad might get clicks but not conversions. CPA is what matters.
- **Not Segmenting Data** → Results look okay overall, but maybe mobile traffic is tanking your ROI while desktop is profitable.
- **Ignoring Placements** → On Display/YouTube, letting ads run on irrelevant sites or videos wastes cash.

Quick Checklist: Top 10 Mistakes to Avoid

1. Only using broad match keywords.
2. Sending clicks to your homepage.
3. Not setting up conversion tracking.
4. Writing ads for yourself, not your client avatar.
5. Scaling budgets too fast.
6. Testing everything at once.
7. Relying fully on Smart Campaigns.
8. Violating Google's ad policies.
9. Killing A/B tests too early.
10. Ignoring device/location performance splits.

☞ Print this and keep it near your desk. It's your "safety net" when running campaigns.

Mini Exercise: Mistake Audit

Take your current or past campaign and answer:

- Did I run only broad match keywords?
- Am I sending people to a landing page or a homepage?
- Do I have conversion tracking installed?
- Did I scale or test too fast?
- Am I confident I'm fully policy-compliant?

Circle the mistakes you've made. Don't worry — every pro (including me) has made most of them. What matters is that you **learn once, fix forever.**

✅ *Action Steps*

1. Run a **mistake audit** on your campaigns this week.
2. Fix the "big three" first: landing pages, conversion tracking, and keyword targeting.
3. Print the "Top 10 Mistakes" checklist for reference.
4. Commit: No more wasted budget on rookie errors.

Policy Reference Box: Safe Words vs. Red Flag Words

Google's ad review system is picky. Sometimes it's not about your intent, it's about the **words you use**. Here's a quick guide:

✅ **Safe Words (Compliance-Friendly Alternatives)**
Use these to stay persuasive *and* policy-safe:

- "Effective" instead of "Guaranteed"
- "Helps with" instead of "Cures"
- "Trusted by [X clients]" instead of "#1 Best"
- "See if you qualify" instead of "Instant approval"

- "Support" instead of "Treatment" (for health-related niches)

Red Flag Words (Risky / Policy-Violating)

These often trigger disapprovals or suspensions:

- "Guaranteed"
- "Cure" / "Fix" / "Eliminate forever"
- "Best" / "#1" (unless 100% verified and sourced)
- "Instant" / "Quick money" / "Overnight"
- "Lose weight fast" / "Miracle"
- "100% free" (Google sees this as clickbait unless properly disclosed)

Mini Exercise: Rewrite a Red Flag Ad into a Policy-Safe Version

Below are 3 example ads that would likely get flagged by Google. Your job is to **rewrite them using Safe Words** while still keeping them persuasive.

× Red Flag Example 1:

"Lose Weight Fast! Guaranteed Results in Just 7 Days!"

☞ **Rewrite with Safe Words:**

"Discover a program that helps you feel healthier and more confident — many clients notice results within their first week."

× Red Flag Example 2:

"Get Instant Approval for Your Loan — 100% Guaranteed!"

☞ **Rewrite with Safe Words:**

"See if you qualify for flexible loan options today — fast online application, trusted by thousands."

× Red Flag Example 3:

"The #1 Best Cure for Back Pain — Eliminate It Forever!"

☞ **Rewrite with Safe Words:**

"Find support that helps ease back pain and improve daily comfort —

trusted by clients worldwide."

Your Turn:
Take one of your own draft ads and check:

- Does it contain a **red flag word**?
- How can you swap it for a **safe alternative** without losing impact?
- Rewrite it and compare side-by-side.

By practicing this now, you'll save yourself from costly disapprovals later.

Types of Evergreen Google Ads Structures

1. Evergreen Search Campaigns (Core Keywords)

- Focus: High-intent keywords that never go out of style ("plumber near me," "buy running shoes online").
- Why Evergreen: People are always searching, no matter the season.
- Best For: Local businesses, service providers, eCommerce with staple products.

2. Evergreen Display Campaigns (Awareness Drip)

- Focus: Always-on retargeting banners with consistent brand presence.
- Why Evergreen: Keeps your offer "in front of" prospects across the web.
- Best For: Course creators, consultants, eCommerce brands.

3. Evergreen YouTube Campaigns (Video Funnels)

- Focus: A 3-part video sequence → Hook (problem), Story (solution), CTA (offer).
- Why Evergreen: YouTube traffic grows continuously, and good videos work for months.

- Best For: Coaches, personal brands, SaaS, any product with a story.

4. Evergreen Funnel-Based Structures (Cold → Warm → Hot)

Focus: Layered campaigns always running in tandem.

- Cold: Search/YouTube for awareness.
- Warm: Retargeting with proof/testimonials.
- Hot: Conversion-focused offers.

Why Evergreen: Creates a predictable flow of leads/clients month after month.Best For: Businesses with long-term growth goals, high-ticket services, coaching.

18

Evergreen Campaign Structures

My First "Set It and Forget It" Win

I still remember the first time I woke up, opened my dashboard, and saw leads waiting for me — all from a campaign I hadn't touched in weeks. That was my first **evergreen campaign**, and it felt like magic.

It wasn't a magic trick though — it was structure. I had finally built a campaign that worked day after day, because it was rooted in timeless human behavior, not seasonal hacks or trends.

That's what I want to give you in this chapter: the **four evergreen structures** you can use to create predictable, compounding results.

1. Evergreen Search Campaigns (Core Keywords)

Search campaigns are the backbone of evergreen. Why? Because people's **core needs never change**.

- A homeowner will always search "plumber near me."
- Someone who wants to get fit will always search "best personal trainer."

- A shopper will always type "buy running shoes online."

☞ Evergreen Search is about identifying **high-intent, timeless keywords** and building campaigns around them.

Framework:

- Campaign Type: Standard Search
- Keywords: Exact + Phrase Match on core buying terms
- Landing Page: Offer page that never changes (only optimizes over time)
- Bidding: Maximize conversions or manual CPC with gradual scale

2. Evergreen Display Campaigns (Awareness Drip)

Display often gets overlooked, but it shines in evergreen mode — especially for retargeting.

Think of it as your **digital billboard**. Even if someone doesn't click, they keep seeing your brand everywhere, which builds familiarity and trust.

Framework:

- Campaign Type: Display → Retargeting audiences
- Creative: Branded banners with consistent headline + CTA
- Placement: Broad Google Display Network with exclusions for irrelevant sites
- Budget: Small, always-on daily drip ($5–$20/day)

☞ Evergreen Display = **low cost, high repetition.**

3. Evergreen YouTube Campaigns (Video Funnels)

YouTube ads are powerful because video builds connection fast. With evergreen, the key is creating a **timeless video sequence**:

- **Hook Video:** Agitate the problem. (Why their current solution isn't working.)
- **Story Video:** Share your unique method or story.
- **CTA Video:** Direct, persuasive, with a clear next step.

Framework:

- Campaign Type: In-Stream Ads targeting keywords, placements, or audiences
- Creative: Pre-recorded evergreen videos
- Budget: Scale slowly, reinvest profits
- Funnel: Send to landing page or free resource (eBook, webinar, trial)

☞ Done right, a single video sequence can run profitably for **months or even years**.

4. Evergreen Funnel-Based Structures (Cold → Warm → Hot)

This is where it all comes together. The most resilient evergreen campaigns don't rely on one ad channel — they build a **system**:

- **Cold Campaigns:** Search/YouTube to capture attention.
- **Warm Campaigns:** Display/YouTube retargeting with testimonials, case studies, or offers.
- **Hot Campaigns:** Direct conversion ads — discounts, free trials, or book-a-call CTAs.

Framework:

- Always have at least **1 cold campaign** running (top-of-funnel traffic).
- Layer in **retargeting ads** so nobody slips through.
- Use **conversion campaigns** to close.

☞ Evergreen funnels = your digital sales machine.

Bonus Checklist: Evergreen Setup Mistakes to Avoid

- ✕ Only running cold campaigns (and forgetting retargeting).
- ✕ Relying on seasonal promos as your main traffic source.
- ✕ Changing ads too often (resetting learning phase).
- ✕ Sending evergreen traffic to a weak or inconsistent landing page.
- ✕ Ignoring compliance (nothing evergreen about a suspended account).

Action Steps

1. Pick **one evergreen structure** to implement this week (Search, Display, YouTube, or Funnel).
2. Write down your **core keywords, evergreen message, or video script**.
3. Set a **daily "set and forget" budget** — even $10/day compounds when it runs 24/7.
4. Commit to running it for **30 days minimum** before making big changes.

Sample Evergreen Campaign Diagrams

1. **Evergreen Search Campaign**

```
[User searches "plumber near me"]↓
```

```
[Google Search Ad appears]↓

[Dedicated Landing Page: "Book Your Local Plumber"]↓

[Lead Form / Phone Call Conversion]
```

2. **Evergreen Display Campaign (Retargeting Drip)**

```
[Visitor lands on website but doesn't buy]↓

[Added to Retargeting Audience]↓

[Display Banner Ads follow them across Google Display Network]↓

[User clicks on ad when ready]↓

[Returns to Landing Page → Converts]
```

3. **Evergreen YouTube Campaign (Video Funnel)**

```
[User watches YouTube video related to your niche]↓

[In-Stream Ad plays: Hook Video]↓

[Clicks CTA → Free Guide/Webinar Landing Page]↓

[Email Capture]↓

[Follow-up: Story Video → CTA Video]↓

[Offer Page → Conversion]
```

4. **Evergreen Funnel-Based Structure (Cold → Warm → Hot)**

```
[Cold Campaign: Search/YouTube Ads]↓

[User visits Landing Page but doesn't convert]↓

[Warm Campaign: Retargeting Ads (Testimonials, Proof, Offers)]↓

[User engages but still undecided]↓

[Hot Campaign: Direct Offer (Book Call, Discount, Trial)]↓

[Conversion → Client/Customer]
```

☞ **Pro Tip:** These flows are templates. Adapt them to your niche — eCommerce, coaching, local services — and you'll always have a reliable "sales machine" running in the background.

Evergreen Campaign Audit Checklist

Run your campaign through these questions. If you answer **"Yes"** to most, you're on the right track:

1. **Core Need** → Does my campaign target a keyword, problem, or desire that people will *always* have (not just seasonal)?
2. **Stable Offer** → Is my landing page/offer something that doesn't change every month?
3. **Consistent Budget** → Have I set a daily budget I can leave running without micromanaging?
4. **Retargeting Layer** → Do I have a retargeting campaign set up to catch missed clicks?
5. **Compliance-Safe** → Is my ad copy free from risky/red-flag words that could get me suspended?
6. **Conversion Tracking** → Do I have tracking installed so I know exactly what's working?
7. **Optimization Ready** → Am I testing one variable at a time (not

rewriting everything constantly)?

8. **Scalable** → If this campaign works at $20/day, could I scale it to $100/day without breaking the flow?

☞ If you scored **6 or more Yes's** → You've got an Evergreen Campaign!

☞ If you scored less than 6 → Don't worry, you've identified exactly where to improve.

19

Integration Options

1.Meta Retargeting (Cross-Platform Reminder Ads)

- Google Ads = intent traffic (searchers).
- Meta = attention + repetition.
- Flow: Someone clicks a Google ad → lands on site → doesn't buy → later sees you on Instagram/Facebook.
- Benefit: Makes you feel "omnipresent."
- Best For: Coaches, consultants, eCom.

2. Email Nurturing (Lead Capture → Long-Term Conversion)

- Google Ads captures the click.
- Landing page trades value (guide, webinar, discount) for email.
- Email = builds trust, educates, and follows up.
- Benefit: Turns one expensive Google click into **dozens of future touchpoints for free.**
- Best For: High-ticket services, courses, SaaS.

3. Cross-Platform Attribution (Tracking Who Deserves Credit)

- Many campaigns fail because advertisers don't know which channel created the sale.
- Example: Google ad → email signup → Meta retargeting → final sale. Who gets credit?
- Solution: Use UTMs, Google Analytics, and CRM tagging.
- Benefit: You scale confidently, knowing which channel is pulling weight.
- Best For: Any business spending >$5k/month on ads.

4. Full Omni-Funnel Integration (The "Triad System")

- Google Ads brings **cold, intent traffic.**
- Meta keeps them warm with social proof and lifestyle storytelling.
- Email builds trust and closes with deeper value/offers.
- Benefit: You're not at the mercy of one platform — if costs spike in Google, Meta + email balance it out.

Combining Google Ads with Meta & Email Systems

My "One Channel Isn't Enough" Lesson

For a long time, I treated Google Ads as my entire marketing system. If I could just nail my keywords and ad copy, I thought, the sales would roll in forever.

But then I noticed something strange: people would click my ad, check me out, and then… disappear. A week later, some of those same people would come back through **Facebook retargeting** or reply to one of my **emails**.

That's when I realized: **Google Ads is the front door, but Meta and Email are the living room where the real trust is built.**

This chapter is about showing you how to combine these channels into one predictable system.

1. Meta Retargeting (Cross-Platform Reminder Ads)

Think about your own habits: you Google something, you click around, and then you get distracted. Life happens.

That's where **Meta (Facebook/Instagram) retargeting** comes in. It keeps you visible long after the Google click.

How it works:

- User clicks your Google ad but doesn't buy.
- They're tagged with a tracking pixel.
- Later, while scrolling Instagram or Facebook, they see your ad again — often framed with more **social proof or lifestyle context.**

☞ The result: They feel like you're everywhere. That omnipresence builds trust and nudges them closer to buying.

Pro Tip:

- Use Google Ads for **intent** (what people want).
- Use Meta for **attention** (where they spend time).
- Together, they form a one-two punch.

2. Email Nurturing (Lead Capture → Long-Term Conversion)

A single Google click might cost $3, $5, even $15 depending on your niche. If that click doesn't buy right away, you've lost money… unless you capture their email.

Email turns one click into **infinite future opportunities**.

How it works:

- Your Google ad drives to a lead magnet (guide, checklist, webinar, discount).
- Visitor enters their email.
- You send a series of nurture emails: stories, testimonials, tips, offers.
- They may buy a week later, a month later, even a year later.

☞ Email makes your Google spend **compound in value** over time.

Pro Tip:
Automate your first 5–7 emails. Make them:

1. Personal story (relatable).
2. Quick win (trust builder).
3. Proof (case study/testimonial).
4. Education (your unique method).
5. Soft CTA (invite to take the next step).

3. Cross-Platform Attribution (Who Gets Credit?)

Here's the trap: Someone clicks a Google ad, signs up for your lead magnet, sees a Meta retargeting ad, and finally buys after clicking your email.

Who gets the credit? Google? Meta? Email?

This is where **cross-platform attribution** matters.

Tools & Tips:

- **UTM tags** → Add tracking codes to Google Ads links so you know exactly where traffic came from.

- **Google Analytics 4** → Helps you see the customer journey across multiple touchpoints.
- **CRM tagging** → Systems like HubSpot, ActiveCampaign, or GoHighLevel let you trace the exact path to conversion.

☞ Without attribution, you might scale the wrong channel and waste thousands. With it, you'll know exactly which part of your system is pulling weight.

The Triad System: How It All Connects

```
[Google Ads → Intent Traffic]↓

[Landing Page → Email Capture]↓

[Email Nurturing Sequence Builds Trust]↓

[Meta Retargeting Keeps You Visible]↓

[Conversion → Client/Customer]
```

Common Mistakes When Combining Channels

- × Running Google Ads without a Meta retargeting safety net.
- × Spending on clicks without capturing emails.
- × Using different messages on each channel (confuses the prospect).
- × Ignoring attribution data — scaling blindly.

Action Steps

1. Add a **Meta pixel** to your site so every Google click feeds your retargeting pool.
2. Create one **lead magnet** and connect it to a 5–7 email nurture sequence.
3. Start using **UTM tags** on your Google Ads links for clearer tracking.
4. Sketch your own **Triad System**: Google (front door), Meta (reminder), Email (closer).

Once you connect these three, you'll notice something amazing: even if one channel underperforms one week, the others keep your system strong. This is how you move from "ads" to a **business growth engine.**

Sample 5-Email Nurture Sequence Template

Use this as a plug-and-play framework to turn your Google clicks into long-term clients:

Email 1: Welcome & Personal Story

- **Subject:** "Welcome! My story (and what you'll get from me)"
- **Content Prompt:** Share your personal journey and why you created this resource. Be relatable, not salesy. End with: "In the next few days, I'll send you tips to help you [desired result]."

Email 2: Quick Win

- **Subject:** "Try this simple tip today →"
- **Content Prompt:** Give them a small, actionable win (something they can do in under 5 minutes). Builds instant trust. End with a soft nudge toward your offer.

Email 3: Proof & Testimonials

- **Subject:** "How [Client Name] achieved [Result] in 30 days"
- **Content Prompt:** Share a client success story or case study. Add screenshots, quotes, or stats if you have them. CTA: "Want results like this? Here's how to get started."

Email 4: Teach Your Method

- **Subject:** "The [Your Method] Framework (explained in 3 steps)"
- **Content Prompt:** Break down your unique process, system, or philosophy in a simple 1–2–3 style. End with a CTA to learn more (free call, demo, sales page).

Email 5: Soft Offer / Invitation

- **Subject:** "Are you ready for [Outcome]?"
- **Content Prompt:** A friendly, direct invitation to take the next step (purchase, book a call, sign up). Position it as a natural continuation of the relationship you've built.

Pro Tip: Write these once, set them up in your email platform, and every single Google click you capture will enter this sequence automatically — turning ads into long-term clients.

Mini Exercise: Draft Your 5-Email Nurture Outline

Grab a notebook (or open a blank doc) and outline YOUR first 5 nurture emails using the prompts below. Keep it simple — just jot a **subject line + 1 key idea** for each email.

1. **Email 1 – Welcome & Story**

- Subject: ______________________________
- Core Message: ________________________

1. **Email 2 – Quick Win**

- Subject: ______________________________
- Core Message: ________________________

1. **Email 3 – Proof/Case Study**

- Subject: ______________________________
- Core Message: ________________________

1. **Email 4 – Your Method/Framework**

- Subject: ______________________________
- Core Message: ________________________

1. **Email 5 – Invitation to Next Step**

- Subject: ______________________________
- Core Message: ________________________

☞ **Quick Win Tip:** Even if you only finish writing the subject lines today, you've built the skeleton of your nurture sequence. Filling in the content becomes 10x easier once the structure is in place.

20

AI & Automation in Google Ads

If there's one thing that's changed the most since I first started running ads, it's how much **Google's AI has taken over.** Back when I launched my first campaign, it was all manual — I had to adjust bids by hand, split-test ads one by one, and constantly watch the numbers.

Fast-forward to today, and Google practically begs you to "let the machine do the work." Smart campaigns, automated bidding, responsive search ads — everything is built around AI.

Here's the truth: **AI is powerful, but only if you train it well.** Think of Google's AI like a Formula 1 car — fast, intelligent, but completely useless if you don't know how to steer.

What AI Can Do For You

- **Smart Bidding:** Automatically adjusts bids to maximize conversions, ROAS, or clicks.
- **Responsive Search Ads (RSA):** Mixes and matches headlines/descripti ons until it finds the best-performing combo.
- **Dynamic Search Ads (DSA):** Automatically pulls landing page content to match search queries.

- **Smart Campaigns / Performance Max:** Bundles search, display, YouTube, and shopping into one campaign.
- **Audience Expansion:** Uses Google's data to find "lookalike" prospects you may never have thought of.

Where Beginners Go Wrong with AI

Here's what I've seen (and, honestly, what I did myself in the early days):

- They **launch a Smart Campaign** with no solid targeting → AI spends money chasing random clicks.
- They use **broad match keywords without negatives** → AI shows their ads for completely irrelevant searches.
- They **trust AI too soon** without feeding it enough data → like expecting a baby to drive a racecar.

AI is only as good as the **inputs** you give it. Garbage in, garbage out.

How to Train Google's AI the Right Way

1. **Start Manual → Then Automate**

- Run campaigns manually for a few weeks. Collect data on CTR, conversions, and keyword performance.
- Switch to Smart Bidding only after you have **30–50 conversions** for Google to learn from.

1. **Feed It High-Quality Conversions**

- Don't just track clicks. Track real outcomes (leads, sales, calls).
- If you tell Google a "page view" is a conversion, it will optimize for page views — not clients.

1. **Segment Campaigns**

- Don't lump everything into one Performance Max.
- Create specific campaigns for specific goals (search → leads, YouTube → awareness, display → retargeting).

1. **Use Negative Keywords & Placement Exclusions**

- Even with automation, you must protect your budget.
- Teach AI where *not* to spend money.

Personal Note

When I first tested Performance Max, I hated it. The results were messy, and I felt like I lost control. But once I stopped treating it as a "magic button" and instead as a **data amplifier**, things clicked.

The moment I gave Google clear conversions (actual sales, not fake metrics) and excluded bad placements, it started performing better than my manual campaigns. That's when I realized: *AI doesn't replace strategy — it multiplies it.*

✅ Action Steps

1. **Audit Your Tracking:** Make sure you're tracking real conversions (not vanity metrics).
2. **Run Manual First:** Don't start with Smart Campaigns. Collect at least 30–50 conversions.
3. **Switch to Smart Bidding Gradually:** Test "Maximize Conversions" or "Target CPA" after Google has data.
4. **Feed the Machine, but Guide It:** Add negatives, segment your campaigns, and monitor closely.

Case Study Niche Options for Chapter 20

1. E-Commerce (Physical Products)

- Example: Online store selling fitness gear.
- Focus: Scaling from break-even to 3x ROAS by using **Shopping + retargeting + email upsells.**
- Why: Readers love seeing how products go from "struggling store" to profitable.

2. Local Services (High-Intent Leads)

- Example: Dentist, home services, or gym.
- Focus: Using **Search ads** + **local targeting** + **call extensions** to dominate a small area.
- Why: Many readers run or work with local businesses, so this feels achievable.

3. Coaching / Consulting (High-Ticket)

- Example: Business coach selling a $2k program.
- Focus: Leveraging **Google Search** + **YouTube** + **email nurture sequence** to warm leads before a call.
- Why: Perfect tie-in with your own course offer (position you as authority).

4. SaaS / Digital Tools

- Example: Project management software startup.
- Focus: Scaling trials → paid users with **cold search keywords + retargeting + onboarding email drip.**
- Why: Shows readers how even in tech/competitive spaces, Google Ads is a growth engine.

(Optional 5th) Info Products / Online Courses

- Example: Small course creator struggling to get students.
- Focus: Using **intent-driven search ads** + **retargeting** + **limited-time offers.**
- Why: Bridges directly into your reader base — they're already course buyers.

21

Combining Google Ads with Meta & Email Systems

My "One Channel Isn't Enough" Lesson

For a long time, I treated Google Ads as my entire marketing system. If I could just nail my keywords and ad copy, I thought, the sales would roll in forever.

But then I noticed something strange: people would click my ad, check me out, and then... disappear. A week later, some of those same people would come back through **Facebook retargeting** or reply to one of my **emails**.

That's when I realized: **Google Ads is the front door, but Meta and Email are the living room where the real trust is built.**

This chapter is about showing you how to combine these channels into one predictable system.

1. Meta Retargeting (Cross-Platform Reminder Ads)

Think about your own habits: you Google something, you click around, and then you get distracted. Life happens.

That's where **Meta (Facebook/Instagram) retargeting** comes in. It keeps you visible long after the Google click.

How it works:

- User clicks your Google ad but doesn't buy.
- They're tagged with a tracking pixel.
- Later, while scrolling Instagram or Facebook, they see your ad again — often framed with more **social proof or lifestyle context.**

☞ The result: They feel like you're everywhere. That omnipresence builds trust and nudges them closer to buying.

Pro Tip:

- Use Google Ads for **intent** (what people want).
- Use Meta for **attention** (where they spend time).
- Together, they form a one-two punch.

2. Email Nurturing (Lead Capture → Long-Term Conversion)

A single Google click might cost $3, $5, even $15 depending on your niche. If that click doesn't buy right away, you've lost money… unless you capture their email.

Email turns one click into **infinite future opportunities**.

How it works:

- Your Google ad drives to a lead magnet (guide, checklist, webinar, discount).
- Visitor enters their email.
- You send a series of nurture emails: stories, testimonials, tips, offers.
- They may buy a week later, a month later, even a year later.

☞ Email makes your Google spend **compound in value** over time.

Pro Tip:

Automate your first 5–7 emails. Make them:

1. Personal story (relatable).
2. Quick win (trust builder).
3. Proof (case study/testimonial).
4. Education (your unique method).
5. Soft CTA (invite to take the next step).

3. Cross-Platform Attribution (Who Gets Credit?)

Here's the trap: Someone clicks a Google ad, signs up for your lead magnet, sees a Meta retargeting ad, and finally buys after clicking your email.

Who gets the credit? Google? Meta? Email?

This is where **cross-platform attribution** matters.

Tools & Tips:

- **UTM tags** → Add tracking codes to Google Ads links so you know exactly where traffic came from.
- **Google Analytics 4** → Helps you see the customer journey across multiple touchpoints.

- **CRM tagging** → Systems like HubSpot, ActiveCampaign, or GoHighLevel let you trace the exact path to conversion.

☞ Without attribution, you might scale the wrong channel and waste thousands. With it, you'll know exactly which part of your system is pulling weight.

The Triad System: How It All Connects

```
[Google Ads → Intent Traffic]↓

[Landing Page → Email Capture]↓

[Email Nurturing Sequence Builds Trust]↓

[Meta Retargeting Keeps You Visible]↓

[Conversion → Client/Customer]
```

Common Mistakes When Combining Channels

- × Running Google Ads without a Meta retargeting safety net.
- × Spending on clicks without capturing emails.
- × Using different messages on each channel (confuses the prospect).
- × Ignoring attribution data — scaling blindly.

Action Steps

1. Add a **Meta pixel** to your site so every Google click feeds your retargeting pool.
2. Create one **lead magnet** and connect it to a 5–7 email nurture sequence.
3. Start using **UTM tags** on your Google Ads links for clearer tracking.
4. Sketch your own **Triad System**: Google (front door), Meta (reminder), Email (closer).

☞ Once you connect these three, you'll notice something amazing: even if one channel underperforms one week, the others keep your system strong. This is how you move from "ads" to a **business growth engine.**

Sample 5-Email Nurture Sequence Template

Use this as a plug-and-play framework to turn your Google clicks into long-term clients:

Email 1: Welcome & Personal Story

- **Subject:** "Welcome! My story (and what you'll get from me)"
- **Content Prompt:** Share your personal journey and why you created this resource. Be relatable, not salesy. End with: "In the next few days, I'll send you tips to help you [desired result]."

Email 2: Quick Win

- **Subject:** "Try this simple tip today →"
- **Content Prompt:** Give them a small, actionable win (something they can do in under 5 minutes). Builds instant trust. End with a soft nudge toward your offer.

Email 3: Proof & Testimonials

- **Subject:** "How [Client Name] achieved [Result] in 30 days"
- **Content Prompt:** Share a client success story or case study. Add screenshots, quotes, or stats if you have them. CTA: "Want results like this? Here's how to get started."

Email 4: Teach Your Method

- **Subject:** "The [Your Method] Framework (explained in 3 steps)"
- **Content Prompt:** Break down your unique process, system, or philosophy in a simple 1–2–3 style. End with a CTA to learn more (free call, demo, sales page).

Email 5: Soft Offer / Invitation

- **Subject:** "Are you ready for [Outcome]?"
- **Content Prompt:** A friendly, direct invitation to take the next step (purchase, book a call, sign up). Position it as a natural continuation of the relationship you've built.

☞ **Pro Tip:** Write these once, set them up in your email platform, and every single Google click you capture will enter this sequence automatically — turning ads into long-term clients.

Mini Exercise: Draft Your 5-Email Nurture Outline

Grab a notebook (or open a blank doc) and outline YOUR first 5 nurture emails using the prompts below. Keep it simple — just jot a **subject line + 1 key idea** for each email.

1. **Email 1 – Welcome & Story**

- Subject: ___________________________
- Core Message: _____________________

1. **Email 2 – Quick Win**

- Subject: ___________________________
- Core Message: _____________________

1. **Email 3 – Proof/Case Study**

- Subject: ___________________________
- Core Message: _____________________

1. **Email 4 – Your Method/Framework**

- Subject: ___________________________
- Core Message: _____________________

1. **Email 5 – Invitation to Next Step**

- Subject: ___________________________
- Core Message: _____________________

☞ **Quick Win Tip:** Even if you only finish writing the subject lines today, you've built the skeleton of your nurture sequence. Filling in the content becomes 10x easier once the structure is in place.

22

Case Studies of Real Scaling Success

Theory is good, but nothing hits harder than a real story. When you see someone just like you apply these strategies and scale their business, it stops being "possible" and starts feeling *inevitable.*

I've worked across dozens of industries, but I want to show you four different case studies that represent the spectrum of what's possible with Google Ads: **physical products, local services, high-ticket coaching, and SaaS.**

Case Study #1: E-Commerce – From Break-Even to 3x ROAS

The Business: A small online store selling fitness accessories. They were running Facebook ads but struggling to profit.

The Problem: They drove a lot of clicks, but most people were browsing — not buying. Their ad spend was break-even at best.

The Strategy:

- Launched **Google Shopping ads** targeting "buy intent" keywords (e.g., "buy resistance bands online").
- Layered in **Dynamic Retargeting Display Ads** to show people the

exact products they viewed.
- Set up an **email sequence** offering a 10% off coupon for first-time visitors.

The Result:

- Within 60 days, ROAS grew from **1.0 → 3.2** (they made $3.20 for every $1 spent).
- Their best seller (a $29 bundle) became the anchor product that pulled in new customers.

☞ **Lesson:** For eCom, Google Ads isn't just about more traffic — it's about catching people *in buying mode.* Pair it with retargeting and email, and you've got a money machine.

Case Study #2: Local Services – A Dentist Who Filled His Calendar

The Business: A small dental practice in a suburban area.

The Problem: They relied on referrals and Yelp. The dentist wanted to consistently book new patients but didn't know how to advertise without wasting money.

The Strategy:

- Created **Search campaigns** for "dentist near me," "emergency dentist [city]," and "teeth whitening [city]."
- Used **Call Extensions + Location Extensions** so ads showed phone + map instantly.
- Added a **$50 new patient cleaning offer** as a compelling CTA.

The Result:

- Within 3 months, the dentist was getting **25+ calls per week** directly from ads.
- Cost per booked appointment dropped below $20.
- The clinic hired a second hygienist to handle the growth.

☞ **Lesson:** Local service businesses win with **high-intent search + strong offer + easy-to-call ads.** Simple, scalable, and devastatingly effective.

Case Study #3: Coaching / Consulting – Selling a $2,000 Program

The Business: A business coach selling a $2,000 mentorship program.

The Problem: Facebook ads brought a ton of leads but most were low-quality — people browsing, not ready to invest.

The Strategy:

- Launched **Google Search ads** for "business coach near me," "how to grow my business coaching," etc.
- Set up a **YouTube ad campaign** with a 60-second personal story ad → CTA to free webinar.
- Built an **email nurture sequence** (5-part) leading to a free strategy call.

The Result:

- Lead quality skyrocketed. Instead of wasting time on broke leads, 80% of booked calls were serious prospects.
- Within 90 days, the coach closed **15 clients at $2,000 each** = $30,000 in new revenue.

☞ **Lesson:** Coaching is about trust. Google captures intent, YouTube shows personality, and email seals the deal.

Case Study #4: SaaS – Growing Paid Users at Scale

The Business: A SaaS startup offering project management software.

The Problem: They had good product-market fit but struggled to scale trials into paid ac
counts.

The Strategy:

- Ran **Search campaigns** for "best project management software," "Trello alternative," etc.
- Created a **Performance Max campaign** focused on free trial signups.
- Added a **retargeting funnel**: YouTube demo videos + case studies + email onboarding.

The Result:

- Trial-to-paid conversion rate increased from 8% → 14%.
- Customer acquisition cost (CAC) dropped by 30%.
- Monthly recurring revenue grew by $50k within 6 months.

☞ **Lesson:** SaaS lives or dies by efficiency. Google Ads delivers intent traffic, but the *real power* is in pairing it with onboarding sequences that keep users engaged.

Common Scaling Lessons Across All Industries

No matter the niche, these patterns kept showing up:

1. **Intent matters** — Google Ads wins when you focus on buyers, not browsers.
2. **Retargeting multiplies results** — most profits come from follow-up

ads.

3. **Email = glue** — turning one click into many touchpoints.
4. **Start narrow, then scale** — don't try to win every keyword/daypart/device at once.

Action Step

Think about your own business (or your client's). Which case study feels closest to your situation — **eCom, local, coaching, or SaaS?**

☞ Write down **one lesson** from that case study that you can apply this month. That's your next move toward scaling.

Bonus: Case Study Comparison Table

Industry Monthly Ad Budget Core Strategy Key Tactics Results Achieved

E-Commerce$ 1,500Google Shopping + Retargeting Dynamic product ads, ROAS 1.0→ 3.2

Local Service $1,000 Search Ads + Extensions "Near me" keywords, call, offer 25+ calls/week $20 CPA

Coaching $2,500 Search + YouTube + Email Nurture. Webinar funnel, story-based YT ads

$30k revenue in 90 days

SaaS $5,000 Search + Performance Max + Retargeting Demo videos, trial → paid email sequence

CAC ↓ 30%, +$50k MRR

Quick Takeaway: The industries are different, but the **patterns are the same**: intent targeting + retargeting + follow-up = scalable results.

23

Building a Google Ads Team (In-House vs. Agency)

There comes a point in every advertiser's journey where you realize: *I can't do this alone forever.*

At first, running your own ads feels empowering. You're in control, you're learning, and you're seeing results. But as campaigns grow — and as the rest of your business demands attention — you hit the limit of your bandwidth. That's when the question arises:

☞ Do I **hire someone in-house** to manage my Google Ads, or do I **outsource to an agency/freelancer**?

I've been on both sides of this equation. Early on, I tried to be the "one-person marketing army." Later, I hired a full-time ads manager. Eventually, I tested agencies. Each option has pros and cons. Let's break it down.

The In-House Route

Pros:

- Full control: They're part of your team and aligned with your culture.
- Faster feedback loops: Easier communication, quick adjustments.
- Dedicated focus: They're not juggling other clients.

Cons:

- Hiring risk: Not every "Google Ads expert" is truly skilled.
- Training time: You'll still need to mentor them.
- Higher fixed cost: Salary + benefits add up, whether results are there or not.

Best For: Businesses spending **$10k+/month** on ads and wanting deep, ongoing campaign involvement.

The Agency Route

Pros:

- Instant expertise: Agencies bring specialized knowledge, often across industries.
- Scalability: They can manage creative, tracking, and reporting under one roof.
- No payroll headaches: Easier to scale up or down.

Cons:

- Divided attention: You're one of many clients.
- Potential for "black box" management: Some agencies hide their methods.

- Fees can stack: Retainers + ad spend = high monthly cost.

Best For: Businesses spending **$3k–$50k/month** who want results without hiring/training staff.

Hybrid Models (The Middle Ground)

Some of the best setups I've seen combine both approaches:

- A **lean in-house marketer** handles strategy + communication.
- An **agency or freelancer** executes the technical campaign management.

This gives you **control** + **flexibility** without overloading one person.

Personal Note

When I scaled past $20k/month in ad spend, I realized I was spending more time inside dashboards than building my actual business. My first hire was an in-house coordinator who managed the basics — then I layered in agency support for advanced testing and scaling. That hybrid setup saved me both **time and money.**

Action Steps

Check Your Spend Level:

- Under $5k/month? → DIY or freelancer.
- $5k–$20k/month? → Agency is often a smart play.
- $20k+/month? → In-house + agency hybrid for scale.

Ask the Right Questions: If considering an agency, ask:

- "Do I own the ad account?" (Always say yes.)
- "What KPIs will you track and report on?"
- "Can I see examples of results in my industry?"

Start Small:

Even if you're hiring in-house, begin with a probation period. Even if you're hiring an agency, start with a 3-month trial.

Hiring Red Flags Checklist

Watch out for these warning signs when evaluating agencies or in-house hires:

No Transparency on Account Ownership

- They insist on running ads from *their* account, not yours.
- If you ever leave, you lose all your campaign data.

Guarantees Too Good to Be True

- "We guarantee 10x ROAS in 30 days."
- Real pros talk about process, testing, and strategy — not magic promises.

Vague Reporting

- They can't clearly explain metrics like CTR, CPA, or ROAS.
- If they confuse you with jargon, they may be hiding poor performance.

One-Size-Fits-All Approach

- Same strategy pitched to a dentist, a SaaS app, and an eCom store.
- Your campaigns should be customized to your market, not copy-paste.

Reluctance to Share Past Results

- "We can't show client data due to privacy" — but also can't share anonymized wins.
- Pros have case studies, even if scrubbed of client names.

No Questions About Your Business

- They jump straight into "packages" instead of asking about your goals, margins, and lifetime value.
- If they don't understand your business, they can't run profitable ads.

Cheap Too Good to Be True Pricing

- $200/month for "full Google Ads management."
- Usually means cookie-cutter setups, no optimization, and wasted ad spend.

Focus Options

1. Copywriting Compliance (Ad Text Rules)

- What words/phrases get ads disapproved (e.g., "guarantees," "before/after," "click here").
- Sensitive categories: health, finance, relationships.
- How to write persuasive ads that stay "policy-safe."
- ✅ Best For: Beginners who just want to know "what can I say, what can't I say?"

2. Technical Compliance (Tracking, Account Setup)

- Why you need correct conversion tracking (fake conversions = suspension risk).
- Importance of domain verification, SSL, privacy policy pages.
- Ensuring account billing info, addresses, and MCC setups are all clean.
- ✅ Best For: Readers setting up campaigns themselves or worried about account suspensions.

3. Policy Pitfalls (Industries, Disapprovals, Suspensions)

- Restricted industries (crypto, supplements, weight loss, adult, etc.).
- How to appeal disapprovals.
- Steps to protect against account bans.
- ✅ Best For: Readers in “grey areas” or scaling accounts aggressively.

Suggested Approach

Since your book is aimed at a **broad audience**, I’d recommend:

- **60% Copywriting Compliance** (because everyone writes ads).
- **30% Technical Compliance** (tracking + account setup basics).
- **10% Policy Pitfalls** (to cover risky niches without going too deep).

That way, readers get practical rules they can apply immediately **and** a safety net of best practices that prevent suspensions.

24

Staying Compliant with Google Policies

If you've ever had an ad disapproved or, worse, a Google Ads account suspended, you know the sinking feeling that comes with it. I've been there myself. Early in my career, I wrote an ad for a client in the health space using a bold "Before & After" promise. Within hours, the campaign was shut down. Not only did we lose time and money, but it also took weeks to get the account reapproved. That lesson burned into me one truth: **Google compliance is not optional. It's survival.**

This chapter is your roadmap to staying policy-safe — so your ads don't just run, but thrive.

Section 1: Copywriting Compliance (The Words That Keep You Safe)

This is the #1 place most advertisers get tripped up. You could have the best funnel, the best targeting, the best offer — but if your words violate Google's rules, none of it matters.

Common Red Flag Words & Phrases

- **"Guaranteed results"** → Absolute claims are not allowed.
- **"Before & after"** → Especially in health, fitness, and beauty.
- **"Click here"** → Too aggressive. Google prefers natural CTAs.
- **"Lose 10 lbs in 7 days"** → Unrealistic or unverifiable promises.
- **"Best/No.1"** → Unless you can *prove it* with third-party verification.

☞ **Pro Tip:** Google loves **objective, benefit-driven language** that feels helpful instead of hyped. Example:

- ✕ "Get rich quick with zero effort."
- ✐ "Learn proven strategies to improve your investing knowledge."

Section 2: Technical Compliance (Your Account Hygiene)

Even if your copy is clean, sloppy technical setups can trigger flags. Think of this as keeping your "digital paperwork" in order.

Key Technical To-Dos

1. **Verified Domain & SSL:** Your ad's display URL must match the domain people land on. No redirects, no shady links.
2. **Conversion Tracking Accuracy:** Fake conversions (or "hacked" setups) can get you banned. Use Google Tag Manager or native tracking.
3. **Billing Info Cleanliness:** Don't play games with multiple credit cards or fake business details. It screams fraud.
4. **Policy Pages:** Have clear **Privacy Policy**, **Terms of Service**, and **Refund Policy** visible on your site.

☞ **Mentor Note:** Google's AI scans your landing pages just as much as your ads. If your site feels sketchy, your ads will never run.

Section 3: Policy Pitfalls (The Industries That Get Watched)

Some industries are simply riskier. If you play here, you need extra caution:

- **Health & Supplements:** No miracle claims. Stick to educational language.
- **Finance & Investments:** Heavy scrutiny. No unrealistic ROI promises.
- **Weight Loss & Beauty:** No "before & after" or dramatic results.
- **Crypto, Adult, Gambling:** Restricted or outright banned in many regions.

☞ **If you're in a grey area:** Focus on *education, value,* and *soft language.* Lead with trust, not hype.

✐ Action Steps: Staying Compliant

1. **Audit Your Current Ads:** Do a quick scan for banned words (guarantee, before/after, click here). Rewrite them now.
2. **Check Your Site:** Make sure you have Privacy, Terms, and Refund pages live.
3. **Run a "Friend Test":** Would a complete stranger feel safe giving their credit card on your site? If not, Google won't either.
4. **Bookmark Google's Policy Page:** It changes often. Stay updated: Google Ads Policy Center.

Bonus: Policy Safe Words & Red Flag Words

Safe Words to Use in Copy:

- "Discover"
- "Learn"
- "Explore"
- "Strategies"

- "Resources"

Red Flag Words to Avoid:

- "Guarantee"
- "Best/No.1" (without proof)
- "Instant"
- "Before & After"
- "Click here"

☞ Swap hype for helpfulness, and you'll be 90% safer overnight.

Mini Exercise: Rewrite a Red Flag Ad

Original Ad (non-compliant):

Lose 20 lbs in 10 days — guaranteed results or your money back. Click here to start now!

Rewrite It (policy-safe):

Discover a 10-day nutrition program designed to support healthy weight management. Learn strategies you can apply today.

✅ Still persuasive. ✅ Still benefit-driven. ✅ Now policy-safe.

By now, you see that compliance isn't about restriction — it's about playing the long game. The advertisers who get suspended are often the ones chasing shortcuts. The ones who thrive? They build trust, stay transparent, and keep Google on their side.

Focus Options

1. Data Dashboards & Metrics (Tactical Focus)

- How to set up reporting dashboards (Google Ads, Looker Studio, Sheets).
- Which metrics to track over time (CTR, CPC, ROAS, conversion rates).
- How to read trends vs. snapshots.
- ✅ Best For: Readers who want hands-on dashboards and love seeing "the numbers tell a story."

2. Long-Term Strategy (Lifetime Value & Scaling)

- How to use Google Ads data to calculate **Customer Lifetime Value (LTV)**.
- Why focusing on LTV allows you to outbid competitors.
- Using data to refine offers, pricing, and retention strategies.
- ✅ Best For: Readers who want to think like CEOs, not just advertisers.

3. Cross-Channel Learning (Google Ads as a Data Source)

- Using search term data to guide **SEO content**.
- Using conversion data to sharpen **email sequences & Meta targeting**.
- Google Ads as a market research tool (discovering audience demand).
- ✅ Best For: Readers who want to see Google Ads as more than ads — as a **business intelligence engine**.

✅ Suggested Approach

To keep this chapter broad but valuable, I'd recommend:

- **40% Long-Term Strategy (LTV focus)** — show them the "CEO view."
- **30% Dashboards & Metrics** — give them tools for daily/weekly control.
- **30% Cross-Channel Learning** — expand their vision beyond just

Google Ads.

25

Ads as a Data Asset for Long-Term Growth

When most people think of Google Ads, they think of **buying clicks**. But the truth is, the real value of Google Ads isn't the clicks — it's the **data you collect along the way**.

That data is your competitive edge. It tells you who your customers are, what they want, how much they're worth, and how to reach more of them at scale. Once you learn to treat Google Ads as a **data asset**, you stop thinking like a marketer chasing clicks — and start thinking like a CEO building a predictable acquisition system.

I learned this the hard way. In my early campaigns, I only looked at CTR (click-through rate) and conversion rates. Those numbers mattered, sure, but they didn't tell the full story. I'd turn off campaigns that looked "unprofitable" in the first week — only to realize months later that some of those customers ended up buying again and again. I was cutting off long-term growth because I wasn't thinking in terms of **lifetime value (LTV)**.

Let's fix that for you.

Section 1: Thinking in Lifetime Value (LTV First)

If you spend $100 to acquire a customer who buys $100 today, you've broken even. Most people would call that a "meh" result.

But if that customer spends $500 with you over the next year? You've just turned that $100 into a 5x ROI.

That's the power of LTV.

Why LTV Changes the Game

- **It lets you outbid competitors.** Most advertisers can't afford to lose money up front. If you know your LTV is high, you can confidently pay more to acquire a customer.
- **It shifts your mindset.** Instead of chasing cheap clicks, you focus on valuable customers.
- **It stabilizes your growth.** You're not living or dying by daily fluctuations — you're building long-term pipelines.

☞ **Mentor Note:** Ask yourself, *"What is my average customer worth in 3 months? 6 months? 12 months?"* That number should drive your Google Ads strategy more than CPC ever will.

Section 2: Dashboards & Metrics That Matter

Now, let's talk practical. How do you track and use the data?

Core Metrics to Track

- **CTR (Click-Through Rate):** Are your ads attracting attention?
- **CPC (Cost Per Click):** Are you buying traffic at a sustainable price?
- **Conversion Rate:** Are visitors taking the action you want?

- **CPA (Cost Per Acquisition):** How much are you paying per customer/lead?
- **ROAS (Return on Ad Spend):** Revenue ÷ Ad Spend.
- **LTV (Lifetime Value):** Average revenue per customer over time.

Tools for Visibility

- **Google Ads Dashboard:** For campaign-level snapshots.
- **Google Analytics / GA4:** For behavior beyond the click.
- **Looker Studio (free):** To build visual dashboards pulling all data sources.
- **Simple Sheets:** Even a spreadsheet works if you're consistent.

☞ **Pro Tip:** Don't drown in data. Pick 3–4 core metrics (like CPA, ROAS, LTV) and track them weekly. The goal is to spot trends, not obsess over daily noise.

Section 3: Cross-Channel Learning (Google Ads as a Market Research Tool)

Here's the part most people miss: Google Ads isn't just about ads. It's a **window into customer intent**.

- **For SEO:** Your best-converting search terms in Google Ads are the exact blog topics or keywords you should create organic content around.
- **For Email Marketing:** Use the pain points revealed in search queries to shape subject lines and nurture sequences.
- **For Meta Ads:** Retarget people who clicked on Google Ads but didn't convert. You'll double your reach with the same data.
- **For Offers & Pricing:** If one keyword drives high-value customers, build more offers around that specific need.

☞ When you start using Google Ads as a **business intelligence system,** you stop thinking in terms of campaigns... and start building strategies that work across your whole customer journey.

✅ Action Steps: Turning Ads Into Assets

1. **Calculate Your LTV:** Look at your last 50–100 customers. What's their average spend over 6–12 months?
2. **Pick 3 Core Metrics:** CPA, ROAS, and LTV are a strong trio. Track them weekly in a sheet.
3. **Cross-Check Channels:** Take your top 5 search queries and brainstorm how they can fuel your SEO, email, or Meta campaigns.
4. **Reframe Your Ads:** Don't ask, "What's my cost per click?" Ask, "What's this customer worth long-term?"

Quick "Data Goldmine" Reminder

Your competitors are probably treating Google Ads like an expense. If you treat it like an **asset**, you'll run circles around them.

Because once you understand LTV, dashboards, and cross-channel learning, every click isn't just traffic. It's insight. It's leverage. It's growth.

Focus Options

1. Funnels & Follow-Ups (Marketing-Centric)

- Show how cold → warm → hot traffic plugs into structured funnels.
- Email/SMS follow-up sequences to recover leads who don't buy right away.
- Retargeting sequences to nurture interest into trust.
- ✅ Best For: Readers who struggle with "lots of clicks, few clients."

2. Sales Process Integration (Marketing → Sales Handoff)

- How to make sure leads from Google Ads don't just sit in a CRM.
- Sales scripts for follow-up calls or discovery sessions.
- Syncing ad targeting with sales conversations (alignment).
- ✅ Best For: Service businesses, coaches, consultants, or high-ticket offers.

3. Long-Term Client Retention Systems (Business Growth)

- Turning first-time buyers into repeat clients with post-purchase automation.
- Using ads to upsell, cross-sell, or re-engage past customers.
- Building loyalty systems (reviews, referrals, VIP offers).
- ✅ Best For: Businesses wanting sustainable growth instead of "one-off" wins.

✅ Suggested Approach

Since this chapter is where you **tie it all together**, I'd recommend:

- **50% Funnels & Follow-Ups** (the foundation everyone needs).
- **30% Sales Process Integration** (critical for high-ticket/service businesses).
- **20% Retention Systems** (showing readers the "endgame" of acquisition).

That balance makes it actionable but also future-proof.

Focus: Funnels & Follow-Ups (80% Core Focus)

This approach would make the chapter a **step-by-step funnel-building playbook**:

- Mapping cold → warm → hot journeys clearly.
- Showing where each campaign type fits into the funnel.
- Building automated follow-ups (email, SMS, retargeting) that catch the "lost clicks."
- Sharing sample funnel templates for different industries.
- Emphasizing the **predictable system** side of funnels (not just scattered campaigns).

Secondary Sections (20% for context)

- **Sales Process Integration (10%)**: Just enough to show readers how a funnel hands off leads into sales calls or CRMs without falling through the cracks.
- **Retention Systems (10%)**: A teaser about how funnels don't stop at the sale — you can also retarget past buyers and build loyalty.

✅ This way, the chapter feels like a **deep-dive masterclass on funnels** (your "signature" framework) while still acknowledging sales & retention without overwhelming readers.

Structure (Balanced Mix)

Part 1: Funnels & Follow-Ups (50%)

- Mapping the cold → warm → hot traffic journey.
- Where Search, Display, YouTube, and Retargeting fit inside the funnel.
- How to design automated **follow-up sequences** (email, SMS, retargeting).
- Examples of simple funnels for eCom, local, and coaching businesses.
- ✅ Core takeaway: Clicks aren't clients until you **nurture** them.

Part 2: Sales Process Integration (30%)

- How to ensure leads don't die after hitting your CRM.
- Aligning ad messaging with what sales reps say on calls.
- Using automation (HubSpot, GoHighLevel, Pipedrive) to trigger reminders and tasks.
- ✅ Core takeaway: Ads don't close deals — **people and systems** do.

Part 3: Retention Systems (20%)

- Retargeting **past buyers** with cross-sells, upsells, or repeat offers.
- Using data to build loyalty (e.g., segmenting by purchase history).
- Turning satisfied customers into **referral engines** with review/bonus offers.
- ✅ Core takeaway: The most profitable client is the one you already acquired.

👉 If you're happy with this flow, I can now **draft Chapter 24 in full** (with the same personal + professional + actionable style we've been using, including exercises/checklists).

26

Building Acquisition Systems

When I first started running Google Ads, I thought the hard part was getting people to click. I obsessed over headlines, keywords, and CPC like they were the holy grail. But then I learned a painful lesson: **clicks don't equal clients**.

I had one campaign that drove over 1,000 clicks in two weeks for a coaching client. The traffic was cheap, the ads looked great, and I was patting myself on the back. But when I checked in with the client, do you know how many new clients they had closed?

Zero.

It wasn't the ads that failed — it was the system around them. There was no funnel, no follow-up, no sales process. We were filling a leaky bucket.

That's when I realized: Google Ads isn't just about driving traffic. It's about building a **client acquisition system** that takes clicks → nurtures them → converts them → keeps them.

Let's break it down step by step.

Part 1: Funnels & Follow-Ups (50%)

Think of your funnel as the **bridge between Google Ads and revenue**. Without it, you're just paying for website visitors who wander off.

Cold → Warm → Hot Funnel Map

- **Cold Traffic:** People who don't know you yet. You capture them with value-driven ads and lead magnets.
- **Warm Traffic:** People who engaged but didn't buy. You nurture them with retargeting ads, email sequences, or educational content.
- **Hot Traffic:** People who are ready. You present strong offers, testimonials, and CTAs to convert them.

Key Funnel Components

1. **Landing Pages:** Keep them clean, benefit-driven, and aligned with the ad.
2. **Lead Magnets:** Free guides, webinars, or trials that exchange value for email.
3. **Email Follow-Ups:** Automated sequences that build trust. (Tip: 5–7 emails in 2 weeks works well.)
4. **Retargeting Ads:** Remind them what they saw, answer objections, and bring them back.

☞ **Mentor Note:** If you're running Google Ads without follow-ups, you're only harvesting 30% of your potential. The other 70% is lost without a system.

Part 2: Sales Process Integration (30%)

Funnels warm people up. But for many businesses — especially high-ticket coaching, services, or B2B — a **sales conversation** is where the real conversion happens.

Sales Handoff Best Practices

- **Align Messaging:** If your ad promises "3 steps to scale revenue," your sales rep better be ready to discuss those 3 steps — not something totally different.
- **Speed Matters:** Call or email leads within 5 minutes if possible. Response time can double conversion rates.
- **CRM Automation:** Tools like HubSpot, GoHighLevel, or Pipedrive can auto-assign leads, send reminders, and prevent opportunities from being forgotten.

Example

One of my agency clients was running ads for a law firm. Before we fixed their process, leads filled out a form… and sat in an inbox for days. Once we integrated their CRM with automated alerts, leads were called within 10 minutes. Close rate? **Tripled.**

☞ **Mentor Note:** Google Ads doesn't close deals. People and systems do.

Part 3: Retention Systems (20%)

The easiest sale you'll ever make is to someone who already trusts you. Yet most advertisers ignore retention.

Retention Playbook

1. **Retarget Past Buyers:** Show them new products, bundles, or upgrades.
2. **Segment Lists by Behavior:** Someone who bought once needs a different message than someone who bought five times.
3. **Build Loyalty:** Encourage reviews, referrals, and reward repeat purchases.

Example

In an eCommerce campaign, we noticed repeat buyers had 4x the LTV of one-time buyers. By retargeting those buyers with a VIP "early access" campaign, we boosted retention by 20% without raising ad spend.

☞ **Mentor Note:** The most profitable clients aren't the ones you just won. They're the ones you keep.

Action Steps: Building Your Acquisition System

1. **Map Your Funnel:** Write out your cold → warm → hot journey. Where are the gaps?
2. **Check Your Sales Handoff:** Does every lead get followed up within 24 hours (or less)? If not, fix it.
3. **Plan a Retention Campaign:** Create one ad or email for past buyers. Don't let them drift away.
4. **Audit for Leaks:** Where are clicks falling through the cracks — landing page, follow-up, or sales call?

Quick Checklist: From Clicks to Clients

- Do my ads flow into a clean, benefit-driven landing page?
- Do I have an automated follow-up system (email/SMS/retargeting)?
- Are my sales reps aligned with ad messaging?
- Are past clients being re-engaged through ads or email?

When you look at Google Ads as just "traffic," you're stuck on the surface. But when you build **acquisition systems**, you create something powerful: predictability. You know that X dollars spent → Y leads generated → Z clients closed.

That's when advertising stops being an expense — and becomes the engine of your business.

27

Turn Clicks Into Clients with Google Ads

Most businesses don't fail because of their product — they fail because they can't get enough customers. Google Ads can fix that. Done right, it delivers the most powerful, intent-driven traffic on the planet. Done wrong, it burns cash fast.

Google Ads Mastery shows you how to stop guessing and start running campaigns that actually convert. Inside, you'll learn how to write high-converting ads, target the right keywords, build funnels that turn strangers into loyal clients, and scale your business without wasting money.

Packed with real case studies, swipe files, checklists, and action steps after every chapter, this isn't just another theory book — it's a playbook. Whether you run eCommerce, a local service, or a coaching business, this book gives you the exact systems to transform ads into predictable growth.

Because at the end of the day, this isn't just about ads. It's about building freedom, impact, and a legacy.

What You'll Learn Inside Google Ads Mastery:

- How to **craft ads that convert** by matching your message to your customer's exact search intent.
- The **3 levels of keywords** (cold, warm, hot) — and how to use them without wasting budget.
- Proven **funnel templates** for eCommerce, local businesses, and coaching/consulting.
- How to set **budgets and bidding strategies** that stop overspending and maximize ROI.
- Step-by-step methods for **retargeting & follow-ups** that turn missed clicks into paying clients.
- The difference between **scaling smart vs. scaling fast** (and how to avoid burning cash).
- Real-world **case studies, swipe files, and checklists** so you can apply what you learn immediately.

"Stop wasting money on ads — discover the proven system to turn Google clicks into loyal, paying clients."

28

Final Thoughts — Google Ads as a Lever for Legacy

When I look back on my journey with Google Ads, I see more than clicks, campaigns, and conversions. I see a tool that transformed my career — and the lives of the clients I've served.

At first, I thought Google Ads was just about "getting more traffic." But over the years, I discovered something deeper: **Google Ads is leverage.** It's a way to take your message, your offer, your impact — and scale it beyond what word of mouth or organic reach could ever do alone.

I've worked with entrepreneurs who were on the brink of giving up, convinced their business couldn't grow. Once they built a system around Google Ads, they not only scaled revenue but also gained something far more valuable: **freedom.** Freedom from feast-or-famine cycles. Freedom from guessing where the next client would come from. Freedom to plan, to hire, to dream bigger.

And that's what I want you to take from this book. Not just tactics. Not just strategies. But the mindset that advertising, when done right, is not an expense — it's an **investment in your legacy.**

The Three Big Takeaways

1. **Intent is Power:** Google Ads works because it taps into human intent. Meet people where they are in their journey.
2. **Systems Win:** Clicks alone don't build businesses. Funnels, sales processes, and retention systems do.
3. **Play the Long Game:** Focus on lifetime value (LTV), compliance, and evergreen structures. That's how you scale sustainably.

Your Next Step

You've already taken action by reading this book. You now understand more than 90% of advertisers ever will. But knowledge without implementation is just potential.

☞ My challenge to you: Pick **one action step** from this book and implement it today. Whether it's rewriting a headline, mapping your funnel, or setting up your first retargeting campaign — start now. Momentum builds when you take the first step.

And if you're ready to go deeper… this book is just the beginning. I built a full **Google Ads Mastery Course** where I walk you step by step, with templates, scripts, and live examples. Think of this book as the map — the course is the guided journey with me as your mentor.

You don't have to figure it all out alone. You can take the next leap with guidance, systems, and a community of people walking the same path.

Final Mentor Note

Google Ads gave me more than clients. It gave me clarity, confidence, and a way to build something lasting. If you use what you've learned here, it can do the same for you.

Because at the end of the day, this isn't just about ads. It's about building a business that gives you freedom, impact, and a legacy that outlives you.

Now it's your turn. Go build it.

What's Next? Your Journey Beyond This Book

First of all — congratulations. You made it to the end of this book, and that tells me something about you: **you're serious about building a business that lasts.**

But remember this — reading is just the first step. Transformation comes from **implementation** and **mentorship.** That's where the real breakthroughs happen.

I want to invite you to go deeper with me. Here are three ways you can continue this journey:

1. Join the Google Ads Mastery Course

If you enjoyed the strategies in this book, the course is where it all comes alive. You'll get:

- Step-by-step video lessons breaking down every concept.
- Plug-and-play templates (ads, funnels, scripts).
- Real client case studies.

- Access to live Q&A sessions with me.

☞ [Enroll Here → www.takshaydigitalacademy.com]

2. 📥 Get My Free Weekly Ads Insider Newsletter

Every week, I share behind-the-scenes lessons, quick hacks, and campaign breakdowns you won't find anywhere else. It's short, actionable, and designed to keep you ahead of the curve.
☞ [Email us → hello@takshaydigitalacademy.com]

3. Connect With Me Personally

- Follow me on **Instagram**: @takshaydigitalacademy
- Connect on **LinkedIn**: https://www.linkedin.com/in/tarun-takshay/
- Or just send me a message at **hello@takshaydigitalacademy.com**— I'd love to hear what you're working on!

Final Word

You've got the knowledge. You've got the map. Now it's time to move. Whether you join my course, grab the newsletter, or simply take action on what you've read here — I'm rooting for you.

Remember: **Google Ads isn't just about clicks. It's about building freedom, impact, and a legacy.**

I'll see you on the inside.

- Tarun Takshay

What's Next?

Thank you for reading this book. If you've made it this far, you're already ahead of 90% of advertisers who never take the time to truly understand Google Ads.

But this is just the beginning. If you'd like to go deeper, here are three simple next steps:

Final Word

You now have the tools to run ads with confidence, avoid costly mistakes, and build systems that scale. Whether you continue learning with me or start implementing on your own — don't wait.

Google Ads isn't just traffic. It's leverage for your business, your freedom, and your legacy.

A Quick Note Before We Begin

Thank you for picking up this book. I wrote it to give you a clear, no-fluff path to mastering Google Ads — but I also want you to know, you don't have to do it alone.

If at any point while reading you think, *"This is great, but I'd love more hands-on help,"* here are a few ways you can connect with me beyond these pages:

Free Bonus Resources

I've put together worksheets, templates, and bonus videos that pair with this book. They'll make it easier for you to implement what you learn.

Want Deeper Training?

This book is the map. If you'd like the guided journey — step-by-step video lessons, plug-and-play templates, and live coaching with me — check out my full program:

The author would like to interact with you and receive your feedback. Get in touch and send him your reviews

www.takshaydigitalacademy.com
www.taruntakshay.com
tarun@taruntakshay.com
www.youtube.com/digitaltakshay
www.instagram.com/taruntakshay
www.facebook.com/taruntakshay
https://www.linkedin.com/in/tarun-takshay/

To know more check out www.taruntakshay.com

AUTHOR :-

TARUN TAKSHAY

Thank you !

29

Conclusion

You've now walked through the foundations, strategies, and secrets of Google Ads. From understanding intent to creating campaigns, from writing persuasive ads to optimizing for results, you've learned that this platform is not just about traffic — it's about creating real connections with the people who need your solutions most.

If there is one lesson to carry forward, let it be this: **Google Ads is not an expense, it is an investment.** An investment into your visibility, your growth, and your future as an entrepreneur. When you treat it with clarity and strategy, the returns are far greater than clicks and impressions — they are measured in opportunities, impact, and freedom.

Remember, mastery doesn't come from reading alone. It comes from testing, applying, and refining. Don't be afraid to make mistakes — each one brings you closer to clarity. The most successful campaigns are built on persistence and continuous learning.

My hope is that this book has not only given you the tools to run ads but also the confidence to step forward with a new mindset — a mindset of action, precision, and growth.

As you close this book, know this: you are now equipped with a powerful system. Use it wisely, use it consistently, and let it become the engine that drives your business forward.

The future of your business is in your hands — and with Google Ads, the world is already searching for you.

Tarun Takshay
Founder, *Takshay Digital Academy*

Epilogue

Every entrepreneur faces a moment of choice: continue struggling in the shadows, or step into the light where opportunities are waiting. For years, advertising was a game reserved for giants with massive budgets. Today, tools like Google Ads have leveled the playing field. Now, even a solo entrepreneur can compete with established brands, not by outspending them, but by outsmarting them.

This is the gift of the digital age. You no longer have to wait for customers to find you by chance. With the right strategies, you can place your message in front of the exact people who need what you offer, at the exact moment they're searching for it.

But beyond clicks and campaigns, this is really about something bigger: **control.** Control over your growth, your visibility, and your future. When you master this system, you stop leaving your business to luck and start building it with intention.

As you move forward, remember — it's not about running "perfect" ads. It's about running ads consistently, learning from every result, and building momentum that compounds over time.

Google Ads is not just a marketing tool. It is a bridge between your vision and the people who are waiting for you. Walk that bridge with confidence, and let your business create the impact it was meant to.

Afterword

Writing *Google Ads Secrets* has been more than a technical guide — it has been a reflection of my own journey as an entrepreneur. I've known the frustration of wasted budgets, the confusion of endless dashboards, and the fear of not knowing whether growth was possible. And I've also experienced the relief and excitement of finally cracking the code.

I share these lessons with you because I don't want you to waste years in trial and error. My mission, through this book and through **Takshay Digital Academy**, is to help you achieve clarity faster, so you can focus on serving your clients and building your dream business.

To every reader who chose to invest their time in these pages — thank you. Your trust means everything. I hope this book gives you not only strategies but also belief — belief that you can build, grow, and scale with confidence.

And remember: this is not the end of your journey, it is only the beginning. Take what you've learned, put it into practice, and let your success story be the proof that smart entrepreneurs don't just run ads — they build legacies.

With gratitude and faith in your journey,

Tarun Takshay
Founder, *Takshay Digital Academy*

www.ingramcontent.com/pod-product-compliance
Ingram Content Group UK Ltd.
Pitfield, Milton Keynes, MK11 3LW, UK
UKHW041351190726
13845UKWH00026B/545

9 789334 415001